Like the nation that it symbolizes, the bold, magnificent Jefferson National Expansion Memorial poses enormous and baffling contradictions. It is a simple, classical architectural form constructed by the most sophisticated modern engineering and technology. It is a national historic site created by demolishing nearly forty blocks of historic riverfront buildings. It is a national park located in the center of a major metropolitan area. It is a civic symbol that memorializes the American political thinker who regarded cities as "sores on the body politic." In short, it is the perfect place for the interested observer to examine critical, historic tensions in American culture. In the words of Mr. Justice Felix Frankfurter, "We live by symbols." By understanding the phenomenon of the Jefferson National Expansion Memorial, we hold a mirror to our own lives as Americans.

The Gateway Arch

The Gateway Arch:

Fact and Symbol

W. Arthur Mehrhoff

Bowling Green State University Popular Press
Bowling Green, Ohio 43403

Library of Congress Catalogue Card No.: 92-73687

ISBN: 0-87972-567-2 Clothbound
        0-87972-568-0 Paperback

Cover design by Laura Darnell-Dumm
Cover photo by Kurt Hosna

Acknowledgements

Versions of several chapters first appeared in the following journals:

Humanities Education (a version of the Introduction: The Phenomenology of Place):

Urban Affairs Quarterly, Volume 24 Issue 1, copyright © 1988 by Sage Publications, Inc.

The Canadian Review of American Studies (a version of Chapter V. The New Frontier).

Contents

Prologue:
Genius Loci

The writing of history is as personal an act as the writing of fiction. As the historian attempts to understand the past, he is at the same time, knowingly or not, seeking to understand his own cultural situation and himself.

Warren Susman, *Culture as History*

Like a silver rainbow glistening upon the Midwestern horizon, the Gateway Arch has always suggested a promise of new opportunities within the constantly shifting order of modern American society. The 630-foot stainless steel Gateway Arch is the symbolic centerpiece of the Jefferson National Expansion Memorial on the St. Louis riverfront, a man-made national park carved out of the city's historic riverfront in honor of Thomas Jefferson and America's frontier experience. This symbolic landscape of lakes and trees also includes the ante-bellum Old Court House where the slave Dred Scott sued for his freedom and one building preserved from the historic nineteenth-century riverfront: the Old Cathedral of Saint Louis. The idea for the Memorial originated during the Great Depression as an urban renewal and work relief project. It became the subject of a rigorous national design competition following the Second World War, won in surprising fashion by an aspiring young Finnish-American architect named Eero Saarinen. The project marked time during the 1950s, while the space age technology employed during its construction in the early 1960s made it a perfect symbol of the New Frontier ethos of that period. In the 1970s and 1980s it became a catalyst for downtown redevelopment, a major national tourist attraction, a fairgrounds for a major media event, and an advertising logo. The Jefferson National Expansion Memorial is and has always been a sign of the times in American life.

1

A startling occurrence of the phenomenon that Swiss psychologist Carl Jung termed synchronicity, a meaningful coincidence of unrelated phenomena, prompted me to explore the meaning for my own life and thought of what one architectural critic termed the "profoundly evocative and truly monumental" Jefferson National Expansion Memorial (Temko, *Eero* 10). An inordinately wet, dreary winter had lingered far beyond the normal return of springtime, dampening both the atmosphere and the popular enthusiasm that typically greets the onset of spring in St. Louis. One morning as I was driving to St. Louis University in midtown St. Louis during the chronic drizzling rain, I happened to glance toward the downtown skyline in the direction of the Gateway Arch.

I was astonished to discover an actual rainbow encompassing the form of the Gateway Arch. Both forms appeared to be integral parts of the ordinary landscape. However, each in its own way seemed to convey a message of promise and possibilities that transcended the realm of ordinary existence. This extraordinary juxtaposition of two highly symbolic forms intensified and multiplied the sense of awe and wonder generally associated with the phenomena themselves. In the words of Mircea Eliade, a scholar of comparative religions, I found myself confronted by "the manifestations of something of a wholly different order, a reality that does not belong to our world" (11). I became determined to understand the implications of this brief but powerful hierophany linking these symbols of nature and American life.

The study of American culture has often been advanced by individual scholars attempting to give meaning to their own experiences. In his famous 1837 Phi Beta Kappa address entitled "The American Scholar," Ralph Waldo Emerson urged persons investigating American life to respect and interpret their own experiences for the new nation. "The poet in utter solitude remembering his spontaneous thoughts and recording them," he remarked, "is found to have recorded that which men in cities vast find true for them also" (312-313).

Several important American historians have followed Emerson's dictum with remarkable results. Frederick Jackson Turner drew upon his boyhood experiences on the Wisconsin frontier to help formulate his paradigmatic thesis that American culture had been fashioned by "the existence of an area of free land, its continuous recession, and the advance of American settlement"; his mythic vision is objectified in the symbolic landscape of the Jefferson National Expansion Memorial. Henry Adams discovered his "historical neck broken" while contemplating the giant dynamo powering the Paris International Exposition of 1900 (382). The overwhelming incident compelled Adams to seek the lines of force which were undermining his eighteenth-century "education" and, by extension, that of the American Republic his family had helped to establish (27). While unloading drums of oil in the Belgian Congo, Perry Miller experienced his "jungle epiphany" that drove him to explain the meaning of America to himself and to others (vii-ix).[1] This book, then, grows out of an American tradition of personal scholarship by seeking to give meaning to personal experience of a major American cultural symbol.

The slow emergence of the Jefferson National Expansion Memorial inaugurated a new image of the city in my own consciousness. Growing up in an old north St. Louis neighborhood during the 1950s, I had evolved a vision of my city reminiscent of a T.S. Eliot poem, musty and decaying, a world of rumbling trollies, crumbling tenements, its Beaux-Arts monuments blackened by the smoke of ancient coal furnaces, "the yellow smoke that rubs its muzzle on the window-panes" (4). I also shared its hazy, Southern nostalgia for the lost civic splendors of the 1904 World's Fair in St. Louis, the Louisiana Purchase Exposition. St. Louis was to my young imagination a city that the American dream of progress had left behind. Slowly, however, two glistening triangular forms began to gracefully embrace the wasteland that had once been the historic St. Louis riverfront.

Construction of the Jefferson National Expansion Memorial on the St. Louis riverfront during the early 1960s inaugurated a massive transformation of both the physical and psychic landscapes of St. Louis. President Lyndon Johnson lent national stature to the new developments. He told St. Louisans commemorating the city's Bicentennial in 1964 that "you chose progress, not decay. And today, you look forward to the future with pride and confidence" (qtd. in Jordan 605). A rising tide of curious citizens visited the gaping hole where the old village of St. Louis had formerly been located. They recalled the city's two hundred years of growth and decline, eagerly anticipating the new order of things. On October 28, 1965, a single, triangular, stainless-steel wedge linked what had been the two separate legs of the Gateway Arch in a symbolic marriage of earth and sky. High atop the gleaming Arch, an American flag snapped smartly in the autumn breeze. In the words of a popular song of that time, the answer was blowing in the wind.

The bright promise of that memorable October day failed to materialize during the 1960s. The population and energies of St. Louis and other aging American central cities continued to flow into their rapidly growing suburban areas. Highly-touted urban renewal projects often failed in apocalyptic fashion. The entire nation watched St. Louis' notorious Pruitt-Igoe housing project ignominiously demolished in 1973 on national network television; even a new riverfront tourist attraction, a replica of Columbus' Santa Maria, sank in the shadow of the Arch. The promise of October 28, 1965 increasingly appeared to be a monumental illusion.

Despite the initial setbacks that followed its construction, however, the Gateway Arch contributed significantly to new possibilities that emerged during the 1970s. Following the construction of the Arch, the skyline of downtown St. Louis erupted in new development as corporations vied for position within the penumbra of the Arch. Older urban areas like

St. Louis began to experience a growing influx of "urban pioneers" hoping to restore historical homes and city neighborhoods.

The Bicentennial celebration held on the newly landscaped Jefferson National Expansion Memorial grounds in 1976 crystallized all these hopeful developments into one transcendent image. Nearly a million people congregated on the Memorial grounds during that Independence Day for picnics, music and fireworks. Steamboats plied the Mississippi River once again as they had during the halcyon days of St. Louis before the Civil War when the Old Court House was a focal point of national politics. A precision Air Force squadron roared over the vast assembly, dipping their wings in salute. Just as they had watched the demolition of Pruitt-Igoe, millions of Americans now followed the local Bicentennial celebration on national network television. The ritual reached its cathartic conclusion as the St. Louis Symphony Orchestra performed Sousa's "Stars and Stripes Forever." Fireworks danced above the shimmering Arch, while nearly a million people clapped and sang in unison. It was Judy Garland in "Meet Me in St. Louis" all over again.

However, the role of the Jefferson National Expansion Memorial as a national park, an inviolate tract of nature set aside from commercial interests, fundamentally contradicts the tendencies of American culture. Like the relentless exploitation of the Statue of Liberty for commercial purposes, the American impulse to "use" everything often erodes the expression of its finest ideals like that Bicentennial moment. In similar fashion, the Gateway Arch has been increasingly utilized for a wide variety of commercial purposes. It has been used to sell appliances, automobiles, newspapers, television programs, even the city of St. Louis itself. Its symbolic meaning to the nation is continually being relativized and trivialized, its relationship to Thomas Jefferson and American westward expansion increasingly obscured and buried beneath the debris.

Over a quarter of a century, the Jefferson National Expansion Memorial has become part of what cultural geographer D.W. Meinig would call the ordinary landscape, yet the meanings of October 28, 1965 continue to radiate like the ripples of a stone tossed into a pond. Historians David Kyvig and Myron Marty have called attention to the value of investigating such extraordinary ordinary landscapes. They observed:

Beyond the serious importance of examining the past of our immediate world to extend memory, understand the contemporary situation, sharpen social, political, and economic generalizations, or facilitate intelligent policy making, nearby history has a further intangible appeal which may be its most notable quality. The emotional rewards of learning about a past which has plainly and directly affected one's own life cannot be duplicated by any other type of historical inquiry. . . . It can be satisfying to feel oneself part of something larger and more lasting than the moment something that stretches both backward and forward in time. (Kyvig and Marty 12-13)

As the paintings on the walls of the Lascaux caves did for primitive men and women and continue to do for us today, the Jefferson National Expansion Memorial continually evokes profound existential questions that stretch backward and forward in time. What is the human relationship to the natural order? How do communities of people understand their collective identity? What role do symbolic landscapes like the Memorial perform in binding a group or nation together? How does American culture in particular understand its place in nature? And how shall we understand our largest national monument, that 630-foot stainless-steel rainbow that one architectural critic christened "the most ambitious symbolic monument yet undertaken in the twentieth century?" (Temko, *Eero* 10).

The Jefferson National Expansion Memorial is "all one thing" as architect Eero Saarinen wished it to be, a marvel of urban design, yet at the same time many different and contradictory phenomena. Folkorist Henry Glassie has argued that if culture is authentic, it will reveal itself in forms "that are themselves revelations of the paradoxes that throb at the culture's core" (16). The Jefferson National Expansion Memorial is just such a form. It is a simple yet classical architectural form erected by means of the most sophisticated modern engineering technology. It is a national historic site created by erasing nearly forty blocks of historical St. Louis riverfront buildings. It is a national park site in the center of a major metropolitan area. It is a civic symbol that memorializes the American political philosopher who regarded cities as "sores on the body politic."

Like so much of mainstream American culture, the Jefferson National Expansion Memorial embodies a bewildering amalgam of Jeffersonian idealism and Hamiltonian economics. Like the union of the two legs of the Arch, it holds these two belief systems together by objectifying one of the most fundamental tenets of American culture: the myth of technological and cultural progress into an increasingly abundant future growing out of the wilderness. It perfectly symbolizes a cultural tradition that denies the contradictory and conflicting aspects of human society and culture by continually projecting them into an idealized future made possible by the abundance of the American land. The Gateway Arch is the perfect place from which to examine the paradoxes of American life that have grown out of our endless pursuit of happiness.

Arch looking northeast. Photograph courtesy of the Jefferson National Expansion Memorial/National Park Service.

Introduction
The Phenomenology of Place

Romance does not creep along the ground; like the memorial to Washington, it reaches upward—a silver thread uniting earth to the blue of heaven above.

Whitehead, *Symbolism*

The interpretation of a major cultural symbol like the Jefferson National Expansion Memorial necessarily involves the study of American culture itself, a complex and difficult undertaking. Unlike small, homogeneous societies such as Bali traditionally studied by cultural anthropologists, America is a modern, pluralistic society characterized by careening social change. It is exceedingly difficult to grasp American life as a whole. However, a holistic understanding of American culture has been the historic aim of the American Studies movement.

In particular, the myth and symbol school of American Studies sought such a holistic understanding of American culture. This group of scholars dominated the study of American culture during the 1950s and early 1960s. Although they produced highly original works of scholarship, their work became increasingly criticized for its over-reliance upon the written word. John Kouwenhoven made this point when he wrote:

The fact that we are heirs to much of England's culture, including its language, does not necessarily mean, as Constance Rourke long ago pointed out, that we have, like the English, expressed ourselves most fully in literature. ("American Studies" 87)

Increasing resistance developed to generalizations about American culture derived solely from literature or other written sources. Few were still willing to believe that such a diverse society

9

could be so easily characterized solely by the writings of a literate elite. American Studies scholar Gene Wise suggested that the student of American culture instead focus upon what he termed "dense facts" ("Some" 517-547). According to Wise, dense facts are important persons, artifacts, or events that appear likely to reveal many of the links between various aspects of the culture in which it exists. Some of these links may include the consciousness of the individual artist or historical figure, the socio-economic structures in which the "dense fact" exists or was created, or its historical references and meanings. This emphasis upon "dense facts" and their layered meanings suggests a perspective very similar to that of modern phenomenology. Several basic phenomenological assumptions underlie this study of the "dense fact" of the Jefferson National Expansion Memorial.[1]

Human consciousness is one of the central concerns of phenomenology. It has also been a major concern of American culture studies since Emerson's 1837 "American Scholar" address. Pioneering American Studies scholar Perry Miller had difficulty believing that anyone can be a historian without realizing that "history itself is part of the life of the mind; hence I have been compelled to insist that the mind of man is the basic factor in human history" (*Nature's Nation* ix). This emphasis on the role of human understanding certainly applies to the contemporary study of American cultural history.

The principal concern of the phenomenologist turns out to be the intentionality behind human behavior. Historian Warren Susman suggested that intellectual historians "would do well to see ideas in things and to see that there is in fact some connection between the most ethereal of ideas and common, even basic, human behavior" (285). It is this type of human intentionality that gives physical and cultural objects such as the Jefferson National Expansion Memorial the various meanings they are discovered to have.

This broad and dynamic notion of evidence especially applies to the phenomenon of a place such as the Jefferson National Expansion Memorial. Sense of place does not readily lend itself to scientific analysis, because it is inextricably bound up with all the hopes, frustrations and paradoxes of human existence.[2] This *caveat* particularly applies to an analysis of the Jefferson National Expansion Memorial, because Thomas Jefferson's dream of a new and virtuous American Republic was always predicated upon his understanding of and dreams for the vast American land.

Even the most secular modern cultures still contain places where that culture's most important values and traditions are embodied.[3] Many of our most important American cultural values and expressions of identity are embodied in special places: the Statue of Liberty, Mount Rushmore and the memorial to Washington cited by Whitehead. Architectural historian Henry Glassie has trenchantly commented upon the phenomenon of our privileged places:

Our American land, too, is an artifact....People, affectionate or rapacious, have made the land their expression, their testament and legacy....The American [land] incarnates history enormously. It speaks, incessantly babbling myth. (33)[4]

Anthropologist Claude Levi-Strauss frequently addressed the phenomenon of place in relation to his study of cultures. He wrote:

A native thinker makes the penetrating comment that all sacred things must have their place. It could even be said that being in their place is what makes them sacred, for if they were taken out of their place, even in thought, the entire order of the universe would be destroyed. (10)

The Jefferson National Expansion Memorial functions as such a privileged place. It was specifically designed to give place to Jefferson's belief in Progress and America's westward destiny. Noted urban designer Edmund Bacon observed that "the design has irretrievably been made to symbolically concentrate this entire force of westward movement as it crosses the Mississippi at one single point, the Gateway Arch" (St. Louis *Dispatch* 27 Jan. 1963). One can see that the Jefferson National Expansion Memorial, too, is bound up in American cultural values and attitudes.

Privileged places such as the Jefferson National Expansion Memorial encompass all dimensions of human existence, emotional and rational, ideals and economics. In contrast to detached and reputedly objective analyses of environment conducted by the physical and social sciences, place understood as a total phenomenon necessarily considers the highly subjective dimensions of human cognition and feelings. The human response to place is poetic as well as analytic in nature. Novelist Edward Abbey's description of Delicate Arch in Utah's Arches National Park provides an excellent example of the phenomenon of place. "There are several ways of looking at Delicate Arch," Abbey writes. "You may see a symbol, a sign, a fact, a thing without meaning or a meaning which includes all things" (36). A similar statement could also be made about the Gateway Arch; indeed, this work in its entirety constitutes such a statement.

The phenomenon of place provides important clues to the values of the larger culture. The rules and beliefs associated with the natural environment are usually more central to the overall world view of the society than those associated with other subsystems (Boorstin, *Lost World* 56).[5] This view was held by Alfred North Whitehead, who regarded love of the sheer geographical aspects of one's country, its whole nature-life, as a critical force in binding a culture together (68). Whitehead's idea about the binding force of nature certainly applies to American culture. In the minds of many Americans, this country was ordained as Nature's Nation; few cultures have devoted as much energy to explaining their relationship to nature.

Many American cultural historians, therefore, have regarded the phenomenon of place as a key to interpreting American culture. Several paradigmatic works in the field of American Studies have focused on place and sense of place in attempting to understand American culture. Henry Nash Smith's *Virgin Land* examined how the American cultural ideal of an agrarian society inhibited much-needed social responses to the impacts of rapid industrialization; *The Machine in the Garden* by Leo Marx examined the transformation of the pastoral archetype under the impact of industrialization in American life; Alan Trachtenberg's *Brooklyn Bridge: Fact and Symbol* compared American rhetoric about nature with the political realities of urbanization.

The study of the phenomenon of place as a key to analyzing culture also closely relates to Whitehead's concept of symbolism. The human mind functions symbolically when one component of its experience (the symbol) elicits consciousness and beliefs about other components of its experience (its meaning). When a place has become as compelling as the Jefferson National Expansion Memorial, the viewer can be sure that it has become the repository of emotionally charged ideas and is being perceived as a cultural symbol. Symbols like the Jefferson National Expansion Memorial are important vehicles for the communication of meaning. They function within their cultures to objectify the important values and attitudes of the culture. In fact, philosopher Ernst Cassirer defined culture itself as the totality of the forms, or symbols, in which human life within a group is realized (*The Logic* 144).

Architecture such as the Gateway Arch is a particularly important symbolic form because of its permanence and high visibility. Architecture can provide important insights into a culture because it is so bound up with the life of the period as a whole (Giedion, *Space, Time, and Architecture* 19). Urban historian Sir John Summerson extended this analysis even further, declaring:

> The urban historian must not be primarily concerned with administration or with the social, economic and industrial life of the city. He will have to intrude himself constantly into those fields to discover causes, incentives, and controlling factors but...the main issue, all the time, is tangible substance, the stuff of the city, and that implies form. ("Urban Forms" 167)

Thomas Jefferson was intensely aware of the importance of such forms to a highly fluid American society. As he created his masterpieces at Monticello and the University of Virginia, he hoped they would serve as models for the new Republic and provide his countrymen with a sense of purpose and order for their unprecedented experience.

American Studies scholar Cecil Tate, in *The Search for Method in American Studies*, further suggested that this understanding of symbols as cultural forms provides the basis for a new American Studies method. Tate regarded the method of myth and symbol analysis traditionally associated with American Studies as more than simply the rudiments of a methodology. He argued that it was the only approach that offered any hope for achieving a holistic view of American culture. While not all groups in American life may have embraced these myths and symbols, all groups have had to confront them in some fashion. The myths and symbols represent central themes of the dialogue that is American culture.

However, the myth and symbol school of American Studies often viewed certain forms or symbols strictly in American terms. This emphasis reinforced ethnocentric American beliefs about its chosen character and its uniqueness in human history. Tate argues that myth and symbol studies should be flexible enough to accommodate the notion that certain forms may grow out of common human experience as well as out of unique cultural traditions. American culture, while certainly worthy of study in its own right, remains part of a larger humanity.

Drawing heavily upon the work of German philosopher Ernst Cassirer, Tate suggested that an American Studies methodology should examine three critical dimensions of symbolic forms. The first dimension involves analysis of *form*, the symbol's basic structure and the role of the individual creator, such as the arch form designed by architect Eero Saarinen for the Jefferson National Expansion Memorial. The second dimension involves analysis as *process*, the evolution of the form within its specific cultural milieu, such as the effects of rapid urbanization upon American attitudes toward nature. The third dimension involves analysis as *achievement*, the cultural meanings assigned to the given symbol, such as the predominant American belief in Progress or the meaning of the frontier experience. This work employs such a multi-leveled approach in its interpretation of the Jefferson National Expansion Memorial.

Although architects Thomas Jefferson and Eero Saarinen both sought to give form to their beliefs about the meaning of American experience, they also recognized and drew deeply upon the vast reservoir of human experience in their search for ideal forms. It is appropriate, therefore, to view a symbol of their lives and work in this larger, more complete, perspective. The purpose of this work, therefore, is to examine the "dense fact" of the Jefferson National

Expansion Memorial as a symbolic American expression of the fundamental human concern to establish a satisfactory relationship to the surrounding natural world: to create a sense of place. Like the memorial to Washington, the Gateway Arch also reaches upward—a silver thread uniting earth to the blue heaven above.

ROMA 1942 XX
ESPOSIZIONE VNIVERSALE

Mussolini Arch. Photograph courtesy of the Jefferson National Expansion Memorial/
National Park Service.

Chapter I
The Arches of Classical Antiquity

[Saarinen] dealt with architecture as symbol.
Robert Venturi, *Architecture and Urbanism.*

A major controversy erupted soon after architect Eero Saarinen's design for the Jefferson National Expansion Memorial was selected as the winning entry in the 1947-48 national design competition. Saarinen's stunning vision of a soaring stainless steel arch arising from a dense forest on a transformed St. Louis levee won unanimous approval from the jury of award, which spoke glowingly of "the profoundly evocative and truly monumental expression of the design" (*New York Herald Tribune* 27 Feb. 1948). On the other hand, his sophisticated modern design also generated highly ambivalent responses. Many local citizens in particular ridiculed the design, calling it frivolous at best or even a giant croquet wicket; others demanded the creation of a more functional "living memorial" such as a sports stadium or heliport (St. Louis *Post-Dispatch* 26 Feb. 1948).

The most threatening criticism of the Saarinen design, however, did not concern its usefulness but its Americanism. This charge was leveled by the chairman of the National Fine Arts Commission, Gilmore D. Clarke, who, in a letter dated February 24, 1948, damned the Saarinen design for replicating an arch envisioned by Italian dictator Mussolini as part of a 1942 fascist exposition. Clarke raised the serious question for post-war America as to whether the nation could in good conscience adopt a fascist symbol after its very survival had been threatened by the Axis powers.

17

This criticism by Clarke, frivolous as it may now appear, penetrated to the essence of the meaning of a national memorial to Thomas Jefferson. It also posed a fundamental question about the relationship between architecture and culture. Saarinen as well as members of the design commission suddenly found themselves obligated to prepare a spirited defense of his prize-winning design. They attempted to demonstrate that the arch form was not inherently fascist but was indeed part of the entire history of architecture. Saarinen demonstrated the difference between his parabolic arch, an inverted catenary curve similar to a suspended key chain, and the rounded Italian arch, which had never actually been constructed. Many contemporary observers regarded the controversy as silly in the extreme; an editorial cartoonist for the New York *Herald-Tribune* depicted Thomas Jefferson chuckling over the furious debate (27 Feb. 1948). The incident is significant, however, in demonstrating the profoundly evocative and truly monumental expression of the Saarinen design. From its inception, the Jefferson National Expansion Memorial has raised profoundly significant questions for interested observers about the meaning of American culture.[2]

Truly meaningful architecture such as the Gateway Arch gives visual expression to a human ordering of reality. It grows out of a fundamental human need for a system of meaningful places, filtering the never-ending flow of images that pass through our daily lives. In perceiving a powerful symbol such as the Gateway Arch, a person experiences an act of identification which gives his or her individual existence meaning by relating it to an entire complex of natural and human dimensions.[3]

As the allegation about its fascist origins indicated, the Jefferson National Expansion Memorial has been such a potent symbol from its inception. It is a privileged place that possesses deep archetypal and historical antecedents in architectural symbolism. This symbolism, like the Memorial itself, emerged from continuing human attempts to create meaningful forms for humanity's evolving understanding of its place in the cosmos.

Much of the evocative power of the Arch grows out of its archetypal form. An interpretation of its meaning necessarily leads back to its origins in prehistory. The whole process of symbolization can best be studied at its simplest levels.[4] The forms associated with magic and religion that have appeared most frequently over the longest periods of prehistory were simple ones in which the part symbolized the whole. The simplicity characteristic of archetypal forms has often been ascribed to the Arch:

The St. Louis Arch was impressive in many ways. One is because of the design, so powerful, so simple.... (Pelli 226)

As his response to the controversy about his Memorial design indicated, architect Eero Saarinen keenly understood the archetypal character of his design. He had spent considerable time conducting historical research in order to develop his design theory for the Jefferson National Expansion Memorial. The important question for Saarinen was:

how to achieve the simplicity of the Washington Monument or the great pyramids of Egypt, because the simplest and purest forms last the longest, and I have always felt this arch of stainless steel would last a thousand years. (qtd. in Dunlap 12)

Because of the elemental quality of its archetypal symbolism, the Memorial elicits many common cultural and human associations. It was not surprising, therefore, that the Jefferson National Expansion Memorial would generate an intense collective response.[5]

The mingling of humanity and the gods with the cosmos itself is one of the prime characteristics of ancient myths and cultural symbols. As Saarinen himself commented, "In a way, architecture is simply placing something between earth and sky" (Temko, "Something Between" 123). Archetypal precedents for the Jefferson National Expansion Memorial exist in such ancient myths about the cosmos. Sacred places originally revealed absolute reality and made human orientation possible within an apparently overwhelming cosmos. The sacred place founded the world in the sense that it fixed the limits and established the order of the cosmos (Eliade 30). For example, ancient Chinese texts explain how one official calculated the exact position of the *axis mundi*, the center of the world, for locating the sacred place. It was found to be "the place where earth and sky meet, where the four seasons merge, where wind and rain are gathered in, and where *yin* and *yang* are in harmony" (Wheatley 152).[6] The Judeo-Christian story of the Garden of Eden provides another excellent example of the mingling of the gods with humanity in a primordial state. Such places symbolized the center of the world.

The Jefferson National Expansion Memorial also functions as an *axis mundi*. It, too, is a privileged place where earth and sky meet in harmony. One Japanese architectural critic noted:

At times when you look at the Arch with the sky as background, it appears almost like a rainbow. It is very fantastic. (Pelli 220)

The image of a rainbow recalls humanity's earliest attempts to interpret the will of the gods in the form of totems. Totemism represented one of the earliest human attempts to order the cosmos and to create meaningful forms for human communities by means of human identification and empathy with the natural world. Early humanity discerned clues from the natural world in order to develop a metaphor, or symbol, for social organization and to understand its place in the cosmos. The totem signified the integrated cosmos and provided a social concept of nature (Bateson 484).[7]

The archetypal totem is the rainbow depicted in the Genesis account of the Flood. In this mythic story Yahweh elects to destroy mankind because of its overweening arrogance. However, He preserves Noah and his family from the holocaust in order to perpetuate the race and to redeem His chosen people. To inaugurate a new epoch and to symbolize His covenant with His people, Yahweh manifests an overarching rainbow which sweeps across the dome of heaven as a symbol of His grace (Genesis 3). The rainbow thus signifies a harmonious relationship between nature and culture.

The motive underlying archetypal symbols such as the rainbow stemmed from the growing human desire in agricultural communities to overcome the randomness of nature and to reconcile the polarities of life and death. Some historians and anthropologists regard ancient myths such as the expulsion of Adam from the Garden of Eden as cultural commentaries. These myths evolved to interpret the revolution in human society beginning with the development of agriculture in the near East. The theme of a garden paradise appears in Sumerian cuneiform tablets, the earliest examples of writing, from around the fourth millennium B.C. Sumer, widely regarded as the seedbed of world civilization, gave civilization the word Eden (Ayensu, Heywood, Lucas and Defillips 29). Continual attempts to create arcadian communities clearly indicates a deep-seated human desire to replace a condition of increasing existential uncertainty with a lost liberty and harmony.

The traditional view of human history regards the ancient Middle East as the incubator of human civilization. Here emergence of towns and cities in Sumeria, India and Egypt accelerated the pace of social and cultural change by providing containers for technological and social differentiation. With increasing human self-consciousness made possible by more extensive human settlements also came increasing awareness of the ambivalence of nature. To compensate for its relative impotence in the face of nature, humanity created symbols to enlist the support of supernatural forces and to enhance its own power to maintain its food supply. Symbolism, then, became an important vehicle of human development. In all human cultures, architectural form became an expression of the culturally perceived relationship between humanity and nature.[8]

The ancient city in particular symbolized the entire cosmos. One of the reasons ancient cities became such potent symbols is that they presented a formal structure in which the highest values were expressed above everything else, such as the Acropolis in ancient Athens. These cities transmitted the message that the human settlement contained a hierarchy of values. As an idealized landscape, a national park and historic site that obliterated the original village of St. Louis, the Jefferson National Expansion Memorial shares many of the basic characteristics of early cities that arose as humanity evolved from its nomadic origins into a settled existence based upon agriculture (Doxiadis 133). The Jefferson National Expansion Memorial clearly demonstrated this deep-seated human desire to objectify a hierarchy of values within the urban setting. Eero Saarinen fought unsuccessfully to establish height restrictions on buildings close to the Jefferson National Expansion Memorial and to establish design guidelines for future downtown development.[9] His overriding concern was always to maintain the Memorial as the dominant feature of the St. Louis skyline so that its role as national monument would not be diminished.

Even modern cities and new towns such as Reston, Virginia that are established *de novo* retain some ancient conceptions regarding humanity's place in the cosmos. For example, many of them are formed in the shape of mandalas, circular forms which symbolize the universe. Not only traditional Peking but the futuristic city Brasilia is laden with symbols that express a common and deep-seated human desire to order the earth and to establish a link between terrestrial space and the overarching sky (Doxiadis 171). The meaning of the Gateway Arch is derived from such ancient archetypes:

Like the dome it symbolizes heaven, the limbs leading the eye upward to the round curve at the apex; and in analogy to the monumental portal that opens into the city or palace it regally beckons the traveler to enter the promised land. (Tulan 200)

The Jefferson National Expansion Memorial draws heavily upon the cosmic symbolism of the dome of heaven, an archetype that appears almost universally in the ancient world. Saarinen had originally envisioned the memorial in the form of a giant dome on the St. Louis riverfront. Describing how he conceptualized this design, Saarinen recalled that:

We began to imagine some kind of dome which was much more open than the Jefferson Memorial in Washington. Maybe it could be a great pierced concrete dome that touched the ground on just three points. (Corrigan 12F)

Saarinen believed that the form of the dome seemed distinctly appropriate for a memorial to Thomas Jefferson. Commenting upon the Jefferson Memorial constructed in Washington, D.C., he observed:

The basic shape does not seem wrong for Jefferson. In a way, it's the same as our Jefferson Monument in Saint Louis—in one case the dome, in the other case the rounded arch. I was thinking of the problem in that way, and only later did it occur to me that it was a gateway to the west. (Temko, "Something Between" 79)

He worked diligently to incorporate the dome of the Old Court House in St. Louis, modeled on the Pantheon, into the landscape design of the Jefferson National Expansion Memorial. The Pantheon in Rome had deeply inspired Jefferson, although he had never actually viewed the structure during his European travels. Jefferson had, however, carefully studied Andrea Palladio's masterful drawings of the structure. The Rotunda of the University of Virginia, Jefferson's shrine to American democratic education that embodies his own highest ideals, was also directly modeled on the Pantheon.[10]

In addition to the symbolism of the dome of heaven, the Gateway Arch draws upon the symbolism of the classical arch form. In describing the design process for the Memorial, Saarinen noted that the design evolved from a traditional dome shape into that of an arch:

We came back to the thought that placing it on the west bank of the Mississippi was not bad at all. It seemed like a sort of modern adaptation of a Roman triumphal arch. (St. Louis *Post-Dispatch* 7 March 1948)

The triumphal arch objectified new human attitudes toward the natural world which evolved in western civilization. In Saarinen's words, the Jefferson National Expansion Memorial would form "a triumphal arch for our age as the triumphal arches of classical antiquity were for theirs" (St. Louis *Post-Dispatch* 7 March 1948).

Saarinen's defense of his Memorial design against the "fascist" charge of Gilmore Clarke depended heavily upon such an historical understanding of the arch form. The Jury of Award for the Jefferson National Expansion Memorial design competition had noted that arches of this type were an extremely ancient architectural form. It cited as one example an immense arch for the palace at Ctesiphon, built by Chosroes the Great, King of Persia, in the sixth century. According to the Final Reports of the Jury, dated March 14, 1948:

Thousands of years before Mussolini, parabolic arches were the preferred form of the world's master builders in Persia, who were able, by 220-640 A.D., to erect a vast and parabolic-vaulted palace at Ctesiphon.

It is in the arches of classical antiquity, to borrow Saarinen's phrase, that one most clearly sees the organic unity and sacred dimensions of the arch form. The gateway archetype influenced virtually every culture in classical antiquity. It originated in a remote past when humanity first began to live in walled cities. Gateways provided dramatic and memorable settings for the ceremonial lives of ancient cultures (Smith, E. 10). The city gates, where power generated at the *axis mundi* flowed out from the confines of the ceremonial complex towards the cardinal points of the compass, possessed a heightened symbolic significance. One historian noted that the sacred gate of Ishtar:

was decorated with golden rosette-stars on a sky-blue ground because the inhabitants of Babylon for centuries had looked upon an arched and towered portal as a celestial form, a replica of the arch of heaven. (Smith, E. 12)

Virtually all Asian urban traditions expressed the gateway symbolism in the form of massive constructions. The size of these gates far exceeded that necessary for the performance of their utilitarian functions. The 630-foot stainless steel Gateway Arch on the St. Louis riverfront certainly falls into this category.

Ancient Egyptians were thoroughly familiar with the arch and the vault forms. However, they only used them where they could not be seen. The cosmic order of the Egyptians, based upon stability and permanence reflecting the geography of the Nile delta, held no place in its architectural symbolism for the dynamism of the arch form (Rapoport 165).

The network of roads, on the other hand, became the fundamental existential landscape of imperial Rome. In such a network, gateways became particularly significant cultural forms. One architectural historian commented:

Under the Romans...in all parts of the Empire...the theophanic implications of the *Adventus Augusti* and of triumphal entries gave a celestial import to the towered portal of the castrum and the triumphal arch. (Smith, E. 10)

The Via Sacra was such a road, marked by triumphal arches and punctuated by a series of sweeping vistas. Another, later example is the Arch of Constantine built in Rome around 315 A.D. By maintaining a center in the midst of roads leading throughout the known world, the Romans "transformed the eternal static image of the Egyptians into a dynamic world where the possibility of departure and return, that is, of conquering the environment, became a primary existential meaning" (Norberg-Schulz, *Meaning* 88).

Early Roman cities demonstrate how architectural elements accumulated over time can evoke a culturally meaningful theme. Like the American conquest of the wilderness symbolized by the Jefferson National Expansion Memorial, the theme of Roman architecture was humanity's conquest of nature while maintaining a meaningful center (Norberg-Schulz, *Meaning*, 84-88). Eero Saarinen's suggestion for creating a greenbelt that would extend from the Memorial to the western edge of St. Louis recalled the Roman precedent.

For Renaissance architect Andrea Palladio, the arches of classical antiquity also symbolized a new cosmic order. In Book IV of *The Four Books of Architecture*, Palladio wrote:

If we consider this beautiful machine of the world...and how the heavens, by their continual revolutions, change the seasons according as nature requires...we cannot doubt, but that the little temples we make ought to resemble this very great one, which by his immense goodness, was perfectly compleated with one word of his.

Following a long hiatus after the collapse of the Roman Empire, the emerging sense of humanity as the measure of all things, as *homo universale*, found its paradigmatic expression in the "little temples" of the ascendent bourgeois city-states of Renaissance Italy. Apotheosis and ascension became important Renaissance themes; the triumphal arch form adapted well to the growing sense of human possibilities expressed by ever-widening exploration of the natural world. Like Saarinen's ideas for the Gateway Arch, Palladio derived his inspiration from traditional classical architectural forms, but his singular genius infused these traditional elements with a modern sensibility.[11]

Classical forms also fascinated Thomas Jefferson, who attempted to integrate them into his own vision of an emerging American social order. "The Jeffersonian God," wrote cultural historian Daniel Boorstin, "was not the Omnipotent Sovereign of the Puritans nor the Omnipresent Essence of the Transcendentalists, but was essentially Architect and Builder" (*The Lost World* 29). Jefferson had carefully read the works of Andrea Palladio and greatly admired the mathematical precision of the "Newton of architecture." Like Palladio, Jefferson believed that the proportions of good building grew out of the natural laws of the universe. He often sketched Palladio's drawings and even based his designs for Monticello upon some of them, especially Palladio's Villa Rotunda near Vicenza, Italy (Dos Passos 66-67).

Eero Saarinen once remarked that architecture should, among other things, "fulfill man's belief in the nobility of his existence" ("St. Louis' Gateway Arch" 1). In this regard his beliefs corresponded closely to those of Thomas Jefferson. For Jefferson, classical architecture expressed a sense of human dignity and a social order as harmonious as that found in the universe of Sir Isaac Newton, a harmony clearly reflected in his designs for his home at Monticello. Jefferson wanted to establish high standards for architecture in the New World with his design for Monticello. No precedent existed for building a plantation upon a mountain, just as no precedent existed for Saarinen's 630-foot catenary curve arch. Jefferson, however, believed that he was designing for the ages, just as in American republican institutions he envisioned a new order for the governance of humanity. Through the Palladian windows of Monticello, large arched central windows themselves freely adapted from classical Roman forms, Jefferson enjoyed gazing westward across the forests and mountains of the Shenandoah Valley onto the new American Republic that he envisioned spreading across the vast wilderness in accordance with the will of Divine Providence.

Historian Henry Adams once wrote that Jefferson aspired beyond the ambition of a nationality and "embraced in his view the whole future of man" (Boyd ix). The American land appeared to offer a Lockean *tabula rasa* for a new order of the ages based upon individual freedom in accordance with the laws of nature. Much of Jefferson's architecture, in fact much of his life, can be understood as a continuous struggle between a classical heritage and the open-ended American future, between the tradition of Palladio and the originality of Frank Lloyd Wright, between a "desire for contained classical geometry and an instinct to spread out horizontally across the surface of the land" (Scully 52). According to Boorstin:

The Jeffersonian sense of tension with nature, of the opposition of man to his environment, had been at the root of his need to reverence the Supreme Workman as his God....For the shaping, subduing, and organizing of the material environment....seemed itself the overwhelming task of the Jeffersonians.[12]

The architectural symbolism of the Jeffersonian National Expansion Memorial as both the dome of heaven and monumental portal mirrors this powerful tension within the mind of Thomas Jefferson, a tension between the stability of classical tradition and his desire to create new forms more representative of the emerging American understanding of the natural world. In the New World, archetypal meanings and forms were rediscovered and taken as the point of departure for radically new cultural expressions. The Gateway Arch, therefore, is not just the dome of heaven. It is also the Gateway to the West.

Chapter II
The Gateway to the West

If we were able to go back to the elements of states and to examine the oldest monuments of their history, I do not doubt that we should discover in them the primal cause of the prejudices, the habits, the ruling passions, and, in short, all that constitutes what is called the national character.

Alexis de Tocqueville, *Democracy in America*

The Gateway Arch possesses deep roots in the evolution of human consciousness. However, the Arch also possesses distinctly American meanings in addition to its archetypal symbolism. Eero Saarinen, designer of the Memorial, expressed this notion in the following remark about its meaning:

The triumphal arch, such as the Arc de Triomphe in Paris, has always been one of the great monumental forms and, it seemed to me, was well suited to symbolize the opening of the West. (Dunlap 12)

The Jefferson National Expansion Memorial symbolizes a uniquely American understanding of humanity's relationship to nature: the myth of technological and material progress in harmony with abundant nature. It symbolizes and grows out of a cultural tradition that denies the contradictory, paradoxical and reciprocal aspects of human society and culture by continually projecting their resolution into an idealized future. The Jefferson National Expansion Memorial is at once one of the newest and oldest monuments of American history.

This deep-seated American faith in progress, as cultural observers from de Crevecoeur to Lord Bryce have long noted, paralleled its unprecedented historical experience of discovering and domesticating a vast, primeval wilderness of abundant natural

29

resources. One of the many tourist brochures about the Jefferson National Expansion Memorial clearly reveals this characteristic American viewpoint:

The 19th century saga of the trans-Mississippi West...the land, its acquisition, the men [sic] who lived the story and its rich significance to our nation...is reborn here below the arching Monument. (Arteaga 1)

This Turneresque interpretation of American history closely corresponds to the concept of *myth*. Myth is a sacred story told of a primal event. This unique event inaugurates a new reality, explaining a people's existential situation. This concept of myth does not primarily refer to conventional religion but rather to the underlying image of the world that a culture shares, their world-view.

Using this concept of myth enables one to understand the Jefferson National Expansion Memorial as a symbolic American landscape. Like all vital symbols, the memorial objectifies as well as participates in the myths of its culture. "The Gateway Arch," as cultural geographer Yi-Fu Tuan observed, "is designed specifically to capture a widely-shared historical sentiment" (33). The sacred story it depicts is the growth of the American Republic, specifically the settlement of the trans-Mississippi West; the primordial event is Thomas Jefferson's "invention" of America as a continental nation by means of the Louisiana Purchase; the new reality inaugurated is the *Novus Ordo Seclorum*, the new American order of natural law and progress; the sacred world is America understood as Nature's Nation.

This mythology also helps explain our characteristic restlessness and constant motion as a people. Prescient foreign observers like de Tocqueville have often commented upon the seemingly endless American attempts to understand their culture in relation to nature. A revolutionary nation of uprooted immigrants needed an ideology that would justify and explain their radical break with traditional modes of living. In the minds of many Americans, especially during the nineteenth century, this nation was celebrated as Nature's Nation.[1] Certainly no American professed this belief more passionately than Thomas Jefferson.

This providential view of nature manifests itself frequently in his thought. In his *First Inaugural Address* he observed:

An overruling Providence...by its dispensations proves it delights in the happiness of man here and his greater happiness hereafter. (233)

This Jeffersonian world-view appears vague only if one searches for its purposes outside the world of nature. Its essential quality was not its vagueness, as many of Jefferson's critics have contended, but its concrete Enlightenment specificity. Thomas Jefferson was determined to find the ultimate purpose of human life embodied in the visible universe. He continually asserted his belief in the inherent destiny of the American people manifested in objects of the physical universe such as the Natural Bridge of Virginia.[2]

An avid student of natural history, that great passion of Enlightenment intellectuals such as Goethe, Jefferson undoubtedly had collected local folklore about the Natural Bridge. The Monocan Indians of Virginia believed the Great Spirit had once caused the 200-foot limestone formation to appear at a time when larger, hostile tribes had imperiled the tribe. The miraculous appearance of the Natural Bridge allowed the Monocans to escape with their lives and culture.[3]

This Monocan legend about the Natural Bridge closely parallels Jefferson's own understanding of American nature. In his *First Inaugural Address* he pointed out that the United States:

Was kindly separated by nature and a wide ocean from the exterminating havoc of one quarter of the globe...possessing a chosen country, with room enough for our descendents to the hundredth and thousandth generation.... (233)

To Jefferson, the arch of the Natural Bridge symbolized a providential gateway into an asylum for downtrodden humanity.

Having rejected traditional Christian dogma concerning humanity and nature, Jefferson sought an equally solid basis for a new American culture. He firmly grounded his Enlightenment cosmology in facts of the physical world such as the Natural Bridge. Nature, Providence, and the laws of nature became interchangeable parts in the *Novus Ordo Seclorum* he envisioned. Because American culture had overthrown traditional attachments to place such as the hierarchical seating arrangements of the parish church or feudal fealty to a lord of the manor, it somehow had to create a new understanding of the human relationship to nature. The "sublime" Natural Bridge inspired Jefferson not only with a sense of the power and majesty of nature; it also provided him with a sense of humanity's proper place in the natural order of the cosmos.

This covenant understanding of nature affirmed throughout the writings and political actions of Jefferson appears directly related to his beliefs on natural law and political theory. Jefferson was one of many Americans of his time, Benjamin Franklin being another, who embraced the physiocratic axiom that "the principle of free government adheres to the American soil. It is imbedded in it; immovable as its mountains" (qtd. in Albanese 122).

One discovers throughout Jefferson's writings a literal belief in an American destiny grounded in the transformation of wilderness into a Republic of yeoman farmers. Jefferson found the emerging industrial cities of England such as Manchester singularly repellant to his agrarian ideology and continually strove to inhibit the growth of an American industrial class. He declared:

I think our governments will remain virtuous as long as they remain chiefly agricultural; and this will be as long as there shall be vacant lands in any part of America. When they get piled upon one another in large cities as in Europe, they will become corrupt as in Europe. (qtd. in Hofstadter 27)

Whether in the form of the Natural Bridge, his beloved plantation at Monticello, or in the trans-Mississippi West he secured from Napoleon by means of the Louisiana Purchase, Jefferson never ceased to envision an order "where as few as possible shall be without a small portion of land. The small landowners are the most precious portion of the state" (qtd. in Jackson, "Jefferson" 1). Cultivation of the soil by independent yeoman farmers in a garden-like setting represented his political and psychic ideal.

However, just as the Jefferson National Expansion Memorial consists of space-age technology sited in a pastoral landscape of trees and lakes, one must abandon traditional notions of consistency when evaluating Thomas Jefferson. "There were deep ambiguities in his thinking, which made any effort at consistency impossible," Richard Hofstadter asserted. "He wanted with all his heart to hold to the values of agrarian society, and yet he believed in progress" (25). Gazing out from Monticello toward the American West, Jefferson predicted that "the progress of civilization would continue to sweep across the continent from east to west like a cloud of light" (Hofstadter 42). In this respect, Jefferson shared the essentially forward-looking gaze of Christian eschatology. However, while in Christianity the soul was not to receive proper recognition until after death, in Jefferson's view Providence delighted in human happiness right here in the New World.[4]

Like the Natural Bridge of Virginia, Jefferson's agrarian Republic of yeoman farmers simply grew out of the natural order of Creation. Architectural historian Allen Temko, biographer of Eero Saarinen, captured this sentiment very effectively in his description of the site of the Jefferson National Expansion Memorial:

The clearing from which the Arch would rise, in single magnificence, was the image of the primitive clearings in which explorers had camped, while the great Virginian— our only architect President, wished them westward, ever westward, carrying forth the destiny of the nation and the world. (123)

To realize his ideal for an agrarian Republic, Jefferson created the township grid system as a blueprint for an egalitarian society. Maps of the Northwest Territory clearly reveal this pattern, which from the air still remains highly visible on the American landscape. Ironically, this abstract and idealistic method of township planning, the embodiment of Jefferson's Enlightenment thought, also proved ideally suited for real estate speculation and civic boosterism.[5] Jefferson's corollary objective of opening the vast continent to oppressed human masses undermined his fundamental goal of a stable agrarian order rooted in an abundant American nature. By liberating Americans from traditional social restraints and ties to place, as well as by encouraging them to pursue happiness through domesticating of the wilderness, the notion of progress introduced a fundamental tension into the emergent American culture. Pastoralism and progress represented fundamentally incompatible visions of America's destiny.

This tension, so noticeable to nineteenth-century observers of America like de Tocqueville as a form of rootlessness, rapidly increased as American society outgrew its agrarian origins. "Americans were such excellent transformers of nature," noted the Austrian critic Francis Grund in 1836, "that no single change seemed permanent; they live in the future, and make their country as they go on" (317). Perhaps his cultural characteristic explains why the wilderness theme loomed so large in the mythos of the young Republic. As anthropologists have long discerned, every culture requires the sustenance of nature in order to survive. In the progressive growth of American culture away from its agrarian origins, a compelling need emerged to create artificial roots in the story of the American people. In the nineteenth century the Jeffersonian credo of progress became a cultural dogma that was continually calibrated to meet the needs of an industrializing nation.[6]

The frontier is the limit, the threshold that separates two worlds—yet paradoxically where two worlds communicate and are transformed. Henry David Thoreau remarked, "We go westward as into the future, with a spirit of enterprise and adventure" (Miller, P., *American Transcendentausts* 145). Bodies of water especially participate in this threshold symbolism. Passage through or across water represents an old and universally used symbol—of starting a new way of life and giving up an old one. As Americans advanced from the deciduous forests of the eastern United States across the Mississippi River into the apparently limitless Midwestern prairie, they must have experienced just such a sense of death and renewal. This symbolism, so pronounced in the landscape of the Jefferson National Expansion Memorial, seems especially appropriate for signifying the historic importance of the river city that was literally the Gateway to the West.

In the first half of the nineteenth century, St. Louis was the foremost embarcation point for exploration and settlement into the tenuously-held territories of the trans-Mississippi West. In his authoritative work on *The American Fur Trade of the Far West*, General Hiram M. Chittenden wrote:

> It is doubtful if history affords the example of another city which has been the exclusive mart for so vast an extent of country as that which was tributary to St. Louis....Every route of trade or adventure to the remote regions of the West centered in St. Louis....Following the lines of trade, all travel to the Far West, whether for pleasure or for scientific research, all exploring expeditions, all military movements, all intercourse with the Indians, and even the enterprises of the missionaries in that country, made St. Louis their starting point and base of operations. The City of St. Louis is therefore in the fullest sense an historic datum for all events which transpired during this period in the vast regions to the westward. (99-100)

Noted journalist William Allen White, writing in 1935 in the St. Louis *Globe-Democrat* in support of the proposal to establish a Jefferson Memorial on the St. Louis riverfront, echoed Chittenden's view that "it was here that the traders and pioneers set out to subdue and people that great area...Jefferson...gave the country the empire; St. Louis made it available for service" (8 Feb. 2B). St. Louis before the Civil War represented the advance guard of American economic expansion and progress.

The small French outpost on the Mississippi River to which Lewis and Clark returned upon completion of their expedition subsequently prospered due to its burgeoning commerce in outfitting western expeditions. Its fortuitous geographical location upon the Mississippi River created a virtual trade monopoly reminiscent of Italian merchant cities. By 1823 St. Louis had already established a city charter. In words reminiscent of Jefferson's description of the Natural Bridge, the first Mayor of St. Louis, Dr. William Carr Lane, proclaimed:

> The majestic rise of our city is morally certain; the causes of its prosperity are inscribed upon the very face of the Earth, and are as permanent as the foundation of the soil and the sources of the Mississippi. (Everhart 643)

Barge traffic and later steamboat operations continued to fuel the city's rapid physical expansion.

One of the selection criterion for the 1947-48 Jefferson National Expansion Memorial design competition was the compatibility of the winning design with the historical Old Court House on the St. Louis Riverfront. The Old Court House had been constructed during the 1840s at the threshold to western expansion as a symbol of the extension of American law and progress into the newly acquired territories. Added to the Jefferson National Expansion Memorial site in 1940, the Old Court House located on the St. Louis riverfront represented the next stage of American progress as the developing nation extended its dominion over the western portion of the continent.[7]

The expansive young metropolis had demanded an appropriate civic symbol worthy of its self-proclaimed role in westward expansion. The Old Court House gave a significant form to these civic aspirations. Like most public buildings of the new Republic, the Old Court House was constructed in the classical Revival style favored by Thomas Jefferson. In its *Final Report* of March 14, 1948, the Jury Award for the 1947-48 design competition noted approvingly that the Saarinen design "by its very form is sympathetic with the Court House dome" (3). As the highest structure in the new city, the bronze dome of the Old Court House was easily visible; steamboat captains utilized it to navigate their course.

Other public figures also set their course by the dome of the Old Court House. Senator Thomas Hart Benton of Missouri, one of the foremost advocates of western farmers and territorial expansion during the ante-bellum years of the Republic, made one of the most dramatic speeches of his long career in the Rotunda of the Old Court House. Long committed to the mercantile interests of river trade as the basis for American prosperity in the trans-Mississippi West, late in his career Benton finally conceded the need for a transcontinental railroad to guarantee future western development. Like the roads linking the Roman Empire, Benton's dream was to knit together the rapidly expanding American Republic.

Old Courthouse 1868. Photograph courtesy of the Jefferson National Expansion Memorial/ National Park Service.

At a national railroad gathering held in St. Louis in October, 1849, for two hours the aging Benton forcefully argued the case for establishing St. Louis as the center of transcontinental railroad traffic. In his oration, Benton, who fashioned himself the political heir of Thomas Jefferson, further extended Jefferson's progressive view of American civilization. He insisted that St. Louis' central position between the 38th and 39th parallels where San Francisco can be located made it the natural focus for a transcontinental railroad. The road would realize the original dream of Columbus for a route to the Indies and would open "the rich commerce of Asia" to eastern farmers. Benton ended his oration by describing a giant statue of Columbus carved out of the Rockies, "pointing with outstretched arms to the western horizon, and saying to the flying passenger, 'There lies the East! There lies India' " (qtd. in Dosch 76).[8] Jefferson's Enlightenment understanding of American nature had been transformed by this Missourian into a Romantic article of faith. However, ante-bellum dreams of progress existed side by side with other's nightmares. Westward expansion and the issue of slavery were inextricably linked. Under the same dome of the Old Court House, the slave Dred Scott had first sued for his freedom.

The creation of the transcontinental railroad network, which Benton had presaged, inaugurated major social and cultural changes in American life following the Civil War. Walt Whitman, self-appointed spokesman for those changes, solemnly declared:

If you want to see what the railroad is, and how civilization and progress date from it—how it is the conqueror of crude nature, which it turns to man's use...come hither to inland America. (Whitman 871-872)

Construction of the Eads Bridge across the Mississippi River at St. Louis in 1874 objectified Whitman's confident assertion. It also significantly transformed the Jeffersonian ideal of an agrarian Republic. The world's first tubular steel bridge, Eads Bridge emerged out of the fierce rivalry between the grids of St. Louis and Chicago for commercial dominance of Benton's beloved Mississippi Valley.[9] Urban rivalries like the St. Louis-Chicago competition stimulated the development of a national transportation and communications network following the Civil War. One journal retrospective proclaimed:

Far more than just a bridge, [Eads] Bridge is a monument to the irresistible forces for national growth, to the engineering vision and indomitable spirit of its designer, and to the ability of a young nation's industry. (Woodward, "The World's First" 8)

Memorial architect Eero Saarinen possessed a keen awareness of the historic role of these great railroad bridges. Commenting in the St. Louis *Post-Dispatch* upon how he decided where to locate the Jefferson National Expansion Memorial, Saarinen recalled:

We began to wonder whether one leg should not be placed on each shore of the river, thus forming sort of a great symbolic arch bridge that ties together the two sides of the Mississippi. . .[but] placing a symbolic bridge between two useful bridges didn't seem right. (7 March 1948 1E)

Eads Bridge also grew out of the historic perception of St. Louis as Gateway to the West that Carr Lane and Benton had earlier articulated. Local merchants facing intense economic competition from Chicago and other railroad cities following the Civil War fervently embraced this article of faith. One St. Louis civic leader grandly declared:

Saint Louis is ordained by the decrees of physical nature to become the great inland metropolis of this continent. . . . Greatness is the necessity of its position. New York may be the head, but St. Louis will be the heart of America. The stream of traffic which must flow through this mart will enrich it with alluvial deposits of gold. (Waterhouse 53)

A bridge spanning this favored stream, therefore, represented a gateway to national union and greatness.

James Buchanan Eads typified the self-reliant Emersonian individual of the mid-nineteenth century. Although Eads had never previously built a bridge, he knew the Mississippi River intimately from his daringly innovative work as a salvage diver and builder of ironclad vessels for the Union Army during the Civil War. Like

Construction of the Eads Bridge. Photograph courtesy of the Jefferson National Expansion Memorial/National Park Service.

Whitman, Eads united the rapid commercial development of the trans-Mississippi West with the Jeffersonian ideal of an agrarian Republic under the banner of Progress. According to Eads:

The world is not ruled now, as it once was, by chivalry....A mightier ruler is monarch of the world now. Commerce is that monarch....At whose command the depths of the seas and the bowels of the earth yield up their treasures. Commerce, the annihilator of space, the builder of cities, and the founder of empires. Commerce, who blesses the broad earth with Peace, with Plenty, and with Happiness. (McHenry 2)

Like Jefferson's Natural Bridge, Eads' arched bridge signified, for the American people, a vision of abundance growing out of the treasury of nature. Furthermore, Eads also professed Benton's Romantic faith in the new world to be created by the railroads, in which the mastery of nature would enable humanity to escape the irrationality of history. Inspired by God's wisdom, he stated in the *Daily Missouri* Republican that man might "curb and direct those mighty currents,....banish from their depths their dreadful terrors, and...make their fast waters the faithful and submissive servants of his will" (13 Feb. 1867 73).

For Eads, as for Thomas Jefferson, God was the Immortal Architect who had formed the world according to natural laws. "The laws which guide an engineer," he remarked, "are immutable, and never deceive. Failures and disasters...result almost invariably from the non-observance of these laws, or from want of knowledge of them" (McHenry 154). With Whitmanesque confidence Eads pronounced the arch form such an immutable natural law, then risked his reputation and personal fortune upon that assumption. "As the strength of the arch is dependent upon its form," he wrote, "it is necessary to adopt such means as will preserve it in shape under all trials to which it may be subjected" (*The Eads Bridge* 78). Constructing an arch bridge on the fierce Mississippi posed enormous physical difficulties. Caissons disease, caused by the tremendous pressure of the river, killed more than a dozen workmen. Nevertheless, Eads succeeded in sinking the piers of his bridge into the Mississippi River bedrock. Like Roman arches and viaducts, Eads Bridge was built to signify permanence and union. One hundred years later, Eero Saarinen also sought a perfect arch form to integrate culture and nature.

Societies continually need to create new symbols of collective identity that combine both tradition and modernity, change and continuity.[10] The monumental arches of Eads Bridge provided such a focal point of tradition and modernity for both St. Louis and the industrializing nation. Eads Bridge provided St. Louis, an historic river city struggling to adapt to socio-economic changes caused by development of the railroads, with a new civic symbol that realized its century-old dream of spanning the Mississippi River and, by extension, the entire continent. The bridge enabled St. Louisans to continue to envision their city as the Gateway to the West.[11]

The entire country, eager to return to nation-building following the Civil War, celebrated the completion of Eads Bridge on July 4, 1874.[12] A fifteen-mile-long parade featuring the U.S. Cavalry from Jefferson Barracks, brewers, bakers, temperance groups and German *musikverein*, wound its way under flags and bunting to a truimphal arch near the portal of the bridge. General William T. Sherman drove a ceremonial spike to commemorate the event. Fireworks burst from the top of the bridge, while steamboats blasted their whistles and formed a rainbow with cascades of water. *Scientific American* proposed the nomination of James B. Eads for President. Architect Louis Sullivan later recounted how he had followed newspaper reports of the bridge's construction, and how it inspired him "to cross a great river, to form the portal of a great city, to be sensational and architectonic" (146).

However, many of the weaknesses in American culture stem from ignoring or avoiding the implications of the fundamental shift from an agrarian society to an industrial nation following the Civil War that Eads Bridge symbolized. Historians such as Frederick Jackson Turner traditionally spoke of a Westward Movement, but American civilization was just as much the product of an Eastward Movement of goods and energy.[13] Economic difficulties quickly bankrupted Eads Bridge, and it was eventually absorbed into the railroad empire of Jay Gould. Completion of Eads Bridge also failed to usher in a fee-simple empire of homestead farms in the trans-Mississippi West. Rather than creating millions of independent new homesteads, extension of the railroads by private corporations into the Great Plains increasingly locked Western farmers into dependence upon Eastern capital and markets. Tenancy increased rather than decreased. The Populist revolt of the 1890s failed to reverse the ebbing fortunes of agrarian America. Henry Adams saw the Presidential election of 1896 between William McKinley and the "Great Commoner" William Jennings Bryan as the last hurrah of Jefferson's yeoman Republic:

For a hundred years, the American people had hesitated, vacillated, swayed forward and back, between two forces, one of common labor, the other capitalistic, centralizing, mechanical.... The issue came on the single gold standard, and the majority at last declared itself, once and for all, in favor of a capitalistic system with all its necessary machinery. (Morison and Commager 361)

The ideal of the American Republic that guided Jefferson and other Founding Fathers disintegrated after the Civil War and began to live more in political speeches and popular culture than in reality. The White Man's Burden replaced the fee-simple empire as Americans contemplated the end of the frontier. In his speech opening the 1900 Republican Presidential campaign, Sen. Albert J. Beveridge declared:

Westward the Star of Empire takes its way...the star of empire, as Washington used the word, when he called this Republic an empire; as Jefferson understood it, when he declared our form of government ideal for extending our empire. (Cherry 140)

This ironic tendency to appropriate Thomas Jefferson as a symbol of the new American industrial order reached a cathartic conclusion in the many international expositions celebrating triumphant American capitalism and industry around the turn of the century. In particular, the 1904 Louisiana Purchase Exposition held in St. Louis celebrated a century of American westward expansion and conquest of the wilderness.[14]

The Louisiana Purchase Exposition revealed the ironic conclusion of Jefferson's ideal American Republic. German sociologist Max Weber, one of the first persons to deeply comprehend the implications of industrialization, was invited to speak at one of the fair's conferences on the problems of the rural community. Weber replied that the invitation must be a mistake. "The rural society, separate from the urban social community, does not exist at the present time in a great part of the modern civilized world" (qtd. in Susman 246). A century of progress had destroyed the asylum of Jefferson's agrarian Republic. Oblivious to Weber's insight, however, the 1904 Louisiana Purchase Exposition marked the origins of the Jefferson National Expansion Memorial. Twentieth-century American society would also have to struggle with the tension of determining where the Gateway to the West was leading them.

Chapter III
The Image of the City

The tourism of the "fine view" infallibly implies a naturist mythology.
Roland Barthes, *The Eiffel Tower and Other Mythologies*

A thorough understanding of a complex phenomenon like the Jefferson National Expansion Memorial requires careful consideration of its local historical context in addition to comprehension of its national and comparative dimensions. Eero Saarinen, the architect of the Jefferson National Expansion Memorial, related an anecdote that provides valuable insights into the urban form and cultural context of St. Louis, the site of the Memorial. Saarinen recalled that when he first began to contemplate his design for the Memorial, he carefully considered what the city needed that would be both beautiful and would attract visitors to the city. "I thought at once of a forest," he recalled, "because cities by their very nature have eliminated most of their forests from their midst. What would be more fitting than this expanse of green for the city's front yard, linking it to the river that gave it birth?" (Dunlap 12). Saarinen's creation of this vast "expanse of green for the city's front yard" culminated the ongoing efforts of progressive St. Louis civic leaders since the onset of the twentieth century to fashion an image of a natural, orderly transformation of an urban society in response to the rapid social changes that have confronted American cities during the twentieth century.[1]

Like most American cities during this period, St. Louis was forced to adapt to the unprecedented social dislocations resulting from the massive shift from an agrarian society to an industrial one. These changes included the development of surrounding farmlands and open space, a rapid influx of immigrants seeking

45

economic opportunities in expanding American industries and the related movement of wealthier families to newer housing away from urban problems, health and housing problems caused by rapid urban growth, noise, pollution and a complex of other confusing issues.[2]

Modernization is the umbrella concept typically employed by historians and sociologists to characterize this complex of sweeping social changes related to the industrialization process. Modernization can be defined as the process by which old social, economic and cultural commitments are dissolved in order to make populations available for new patterns of socialization and behavior. These new patterns of modern twentieth-century American life included mechanization, displacement from farm communities, growth of mass media, a consumer economy and especially urbanization.[3]

Modernization can be perceived either in terms of radical change or of cultural continuity. It causes old cultural traditions and symbols either to be discarded or incorporated into new symbolic contexts in order to enable members of the society to understand their experience. If one defines culture in Cassirer's terms as a universe of socially accepted symbols, then modernization means that traditional symbols will have to evolve in response to new collective social experiences. Eero Saarinen correctly gauged the signifying system of the St. Louis community in his design for the Memorial. As the architectural critic of the St. Louis *Post-Dispatch* later reflected:

The strength of this great form [the Gateway Arch] is indicated by the hold it exerted upon the community consciousness for so long before it had the slightest beginning as a physical fact. (McCue 13G)

Modernization, however, does not represent a static condition. The new form that results from this process still possesses the same underlying tensions as its predecessor. Symbolic anthropologist Roy Wagner suggested an intriguing analysis of the tension underlying the forms of modern urban America. According to Wagner:

Whenever a society composed of classes or segments standing in a dialectical relationship to one another...attempts to mediate that relationship through a linear, nondialectical ideology (e.g., Progress), a disharmony is set up that works to resolve itself. (Wagner 127)

American cities are classic examples of this "masking" process, hiding social tensions under the banner of Progress. The rapid growth of cities during the late nineteenth century created the social inequalities that Jefferson had dreaded. The American tendency since Thomas Jefferson has been to identify "the city" as the cause of social problems more properly attributed to changing economic patterns.[4] The idea of park-like settings and expanses of natural greenery to beautify the urban environment, a central feature of a widespread urban middle-class response to rapid social change, is clearly part of a deep-seated American cultural tradition.

American city planning in particular has traditionally emphasized civic beautification, public monuments and parks as its preferred solution for urban problems. From the romantic parks of Frederick Law Olmsted in the nineteenth century to the urban renewal projects of the 1950s and 1960s, progressive civic leaders have stressed physical solutions to American urban problems rather than public controls over private investment and land use decisions.[5]

The initial proposal for a riverfront memorial to Thomas Jefferson reflected the concerns of progressive civic leaders about the squalid conditions that accompanied the industrial expansion of St. Louis. For example, construction of Eads Bridge in 1874 had exerted a major impact upon the urban form of St. Louis. Although the center of local business had traditionally been the historic riverfront, the site of the original village, completion of the Eads Bridge diminished the role of river trade and enabled businesses to move away from the densely-developed riverfront to newer quarters in the western section of downtown. Because it no longer represented the focal point of local progress, the historic riverfront suffered disinvestment and became perceived as an urban problem.

The first recorded suggestion for a riverfront memorial to Jefferson came, ironically enough, from Republican Senator James G. Blaine. In a speech on the floor of the Merchants' Exchange Building in St. Louis on March 31, 1887, Blaine chided local Democrats for the lack of a Jefferson statue in the city (*Daily Missouri Republican* 1 April 1887). The second mention of a riverfront memorial to Jefferson was made by a Confederate Army veteran, Major Charles C. Rainwater, engineer of the local Merchants' Bridge. Rainwater's speech finally stimulated local improvement efforts (*Daily Missouri Republican* 18 July 1888).

Local merchants held an organizational meeting on July 17, 1888 at the Southern Hotel near the riverfront. Their major concern was how to address the growing problem posed by the declining riverfront. The specific object of the meeting was to form a stock company or association of property holders that "could check the serious deterioration in value of the property located in that district and adopt measures by means of which former values might be brought back to the district" (Bryan 1). Despite their efforts, however, the old riverfront district and the memorial concept lagged until the turn of the century.

The idea of a riverfront memorial to Thomas Jefferson was resurrected during the civic boosterism surrounding the 1904 Louisiana Purchase Exposition held in St. Louis. International expositions like the 1904 World's Fair advertised national and civic progress both at home and abroad. St. Louis was preparing its mammoth exposition in order to commemorate the centennial anniversary of the Louisiana Purchase from Napoleon by Jefferson in 1803, as well as to keep pace with its urban rivals like Chicago with its celebrated Columbian Exposition. As one Progressive journal, *The Chautauquan*, reported:

The discussion of the project naturally called the attention of all good citizens to the prime necessity of making the city itself a striking feature of the show prepared for the nations of the earth. (McCall 405)

A widespread movement for civic reform swept the country during the exposition era of the late nineteenth and early twentieth centuries. A group of prominent St. Louis civic leaders who shared this image of urban optimism organized the Civic Improvement League in 1902 as the local branch of the American League for Civic Improvement. The *Chautauquan* reported:

A few persons studied the general subject of the City Beautiful....Organization was promptly effected, and in a short time the Civic Improvement League was actually working. (McCall 407)

The City Beautiful Movement was a middle-class effort to organize and control the new American industrial cities. One of its major concerns was to restrain the spread of inner-city slums, the dwellings of the vicious and depraved, from business and residential districts. In its 1907 report containing the League's proposal for a riverfront park, the League reported that as to the riverfront:

The report calls attention to the present deplorable condition—the familiar municipal story in America: a noble site, almost abandoned by business, the city turning its back upon it and it becoming a resort of the vicious and depraved. ("The City Plan Report" 1544)

The civic reform movement was led by members of the newly-emerging urban middle class such as attorneys, doctors, educators and other professionals. The Civic Improvement League regarded itself as a business organization, doing its work purely on a business basis and appealing successfully for support to the city's wealthy and influential. For example, the League's plan for the St. Louis riverfront, prepared in 1907, concluded that a city "is a great business establishment in which thousands of stockholders are interested" (*A City Plan* 9). Members of the League described the city as "nothing more than a great business institution wherein the human factor plays a leading part" (*The Problems* xxii).

It was the "agitation," to borrow a popular phrase of the period, from the Civic Improvement League that first brought the idea of a Jefferson Memorial on the St. Louis riverfront to the attention

Source: 1907 City Plan Report. Photograph courtesy of the Jefferson National Expansion Memorial/National Park Service.

of the general public. *The Chautauquan* reported that "the desire for a better city to live in finds expression in agitation for a...park on the city's riverfront" (McCall 406). The idea of a riverfront memorial to Jefferson was first put forward by civic leaders as a solution to the physical deterioration of the riverfront commercial district. After the completion of the Louisiana Purchase Exposition, the Civic Improvement League organized a voluntary City Plan Commission to continue and rationalize its work. The League engaged George E. Kessler, the chief landscape artist of the Exposition, as its professional adviser. As Eero Saarinen would advocate some forty years later, Kessler urged the creation of a park on the site of the original village of St. Louis (Bryan 4).

The ascendent middle classes in Europe and the United States were busily involved at this time in physically and culturally transforming their cities.[6] The Civic Improvement League of St. Louis drew upon the examples of similar city plans such as Baron Haussmann's broad Paris boulevards, the Vienna Ringstrasse designed by Camillo Sitte and the monumental transformation of the nation's capital being carried out at that time. The plan:

Recommended that the city widen Chestnut Street to 150 feet from the Union station to the municipal buildings group and develop it like the Champs Elysees. ("The City Plan Report" 1545)

Old symbols were thus being transformed to accommodate the new industrial city. The city plan for the St. Louis riverfront called for a large public park featuring a monumental sculpture as the focal point to memorialize westward-bound pioneers. The dream of escaping the city and its complexities was now to feed the city's commercial development. The plan concluded:

Riverfront improvements are not antagonistic to the commercial development of a metropolis. In the case of this city it would be an actual material benefit to commerce. Saint Louis now has an opportunity of improving a naturally beautiful waterfront without interfering in the least with her rapid commercial and industrial development. (Civic League, *A City Plan* 74)

Although it was widely applauded by the press and general public, the 1907 riverfront plan remained only a vision for decades.

The City Plan Association carried on the work of the Civic Improvement League. The form of the new organization was approved at a meeting held on March 24, 1910. The meeting was duly attended by:

Twenty-five gentlemen [sic] who were interested in the civic advancement of the city. It was earnestly desired...to faithfully represent the best and most advanced public spirit. (Association Report 4)

These progressive civic leaders called for a special effort at "civic adornment," in their words, to make a highly favorable impression upon people passing through St. Louis on passenger railroads. Landscape architect George Kessler prepared a more elaborate plan of civic adornments and presented it to the Plan Commission in June, 1915 (Bryan 4). His new plan featured a broad mall extending from the central riverfront, passing westward along Market Street to provide a distinguished plaza for the Union Station railroad terminal, then continuing westward. Eero Saarinen would later suggest a similar broad green vista to complement the view from the Jefferson National Expansion Memorial.

Subsequent plans for the central riverfront shared many of the elements of the early plans. However, plans following World War One also reflected mounting concern by city planners about the disruptive impacts of the swarms of automobiles jamming the downtown commercial district. One planning document noted that:

The extreme narrowness of these riverfront streets for modern city use has contributed probably as much, if not more than, the decline of river traffic, to the apparent idleness which today distinguishes this part of our city. (City Plan Commission, *Problems* 2)

The City Plan Commission produced its *Plan for the Central Riverfront* in 1928. This document recalled the major elements of the earlier plans but focused much of its own analysis upon the critical need to provide additional parking for the throngs of motorists now congesting the downtown area. "The same forces contributing to the decline of the property between Third Street and the river [the central riverfront]," the plan predicted, "will, in the future, operate to depreciate the eastern end of the present business district unless something more than ordinary measures are undertaken to forestall it" (*A Plan* 2).

Harland Bartholomew, the chief engineer for the City of St. Louis, presented the City Plan Commission with the elaborate plan for redevelopment of the Central Riverfront at an estimated cost of $50,000,000. Luther Ely Smith, the prominent local attorney and civic leader who had been actively involved in previous efforts at civic beautification, now chaired the voluntary Citizens' City Plan Commission. The Plan Commission authorized a large plaster model of the proposed plan to be developed for public display in order to generate support for the planned improvement (Bryan 4). As the *Plan for the Central Riverfront* observed:

In dealing with an area of such magnitude there are encountered problems which go the very roots of the growth and development of the entire city and region. Any plan which will satisfy the popular demand for improved appearance will require large expenditure. To justify such large expenditure the plan should serve some great, useful public purpose. (Bryan 4)

However, it required the Great Depression, not a plaster model, to effectively demonstrate the useful public purpose of a riverfront memorial to Thomas Jefferson.

"I have heard so much about getting back to the old Jefferson principles," quipped humorist Will Rogers, "that, being an amateur, I am in doubt as to why they left them in the first place" (qtd. in Peterson 354). Many Americans during the Great Depression undoubtedly shared Roger's puzzlement, if not his sense of humor, about the elusive American pursuit of Happiness. Widespread unemployment, homelessness, labor unrest and Dust Bowl conditions realized Jefferson's worst fears for the American Republic. In Daniel Boorstin's words:

As Americans felt more entangled with their cities...they were bewildered over what they had lost, and they wondered where urban community could be rediscovered. Was the modern American city to be a twentieth-century American West, with its own special vagueness, its own mysteries, its own false promises? (*The Americans* 246)

Source: 1928 City Plan. Photograph courtesy of the Jefferson National Expansion Memorial/National Park Service.

The St. Louis riverfront, the long-proposed site for the Jefferson Memorial, had instead deteriorated by this time into one of the nation's largest Hoovervilles.[7] The Great Depression threatened not only the dream of Thomas Jefferson but the very survival of American society.

The Jefferson National Expansion Memorial project offers an excellent example of the American myth of progress. In the form of the Memorial, both St. Louis and the nation utilized traditional symbols in order to help resolve the unprecedented tensions posed by the Great Depression for American society and culture. For example, in 1933 a St. Louis high school student, asked by her teacher to depict the city of the future, drew a picture of a downtown skyline that bears a striking resemblance to the contemporary St. Louis downtown—complete with an arch. In the upper left corner, she included the lines from Tennyson's poem, "Ulysses" that led her to select an arch as the dominant symbol:

Yet all experience is an arch wherethro' gleams that untraveled world whose margin fades for ever and for ever when I move. ("Way Back")

The same mythic process occurred on other levels. Speaking on behalf of the memorial to Jefferson proposed by St. Louis civic leaders to New Deal officials, William Allen White editorialized without any apparent sense of irony:

Without the ever-opening cornucopia of wealth and opportunity which came from the Louisiana Purchase our restricted nation would inevitably have made a mockery of Jefferson's ideals. (qtd. in Jefferson National Expansion Memorial Association, *Record* 24)

"The use of a frontier past and its extension into the present and future," observed one historian, "mark a central cluster of images applied in defense of the processes of American enterprise in the twentieth century" (Susman 32).

The image of Thomas Jefferson especially demonstrated such protean qualities during the Depression era. For example, Jefferson demonstrated considerable political value to the Roosevelt administration. On one occasion Roosevelt wrote to his adviser, E.M. House, in advance of the Jefferson Day dinner in 1934 that:

As much as we love Jefferson...we should celebrate him not as the founder and philosopher of the Democratic party but as the supreme spirit of American liberalism and progress. (qtd. in Peterson 363)

The patrician Roosevelt in particular seemed to regard Jefferson as his political model. Restoration of Jefferson's home at Monticello became an ongoing personal interest of the President. In addition to authorizing the Jefferson National Expansion Memorial in St. Louis, Roosevelt also promoted the construction of the Jefferson Memorial in Washington, D.C., as well as authorizing the Jefferson nickel and the three-cent stamp.

There were, however, competing interpretations of the meaning of Jeffersonian ideals which emerged during this period. One group, typically referred to as the Southern Agrarians, drew heavily upon the strongly anti-urban sentiment found in Jefferson's writings for their social and political theory. They defined democracy as an unmixed agrarian economy, local and regional autonomy in opposition to control by large corporations and broadly diffused land ownership as "keystone of the arch" (Peterson 364). Frank Lloyd Wright's visionary Broadacre City, which advocated abolition of large cities and broad distribution of clear titles to tracts of land, shared many of these elements of the Southern Agrarian philosophy.

Most Americans, however, continued to emphasize the progressive economic aspects of Jeffersonian democracy instead of his deep-rooted attachments to the land. Echoing the sentiments expressed by Roosevelt and William Allen White, one local civic organization declared:

The return of the emphasis to the riverfront can be a powerful factor in progressive development of downtown Saint Louis—reversing the tide of commercial building westward of the present "dead" sections of the city. (qtd. in "Progress Report" 18)

Like earlier proposals for a riverfront memorial park, the proposal for the Jefferson National Expansion Memorial also grew out of widespread concerns by local civic leaders about the future survival of downtown businesses and commerce. St. Louis attorney Luther Ely Smith, former chairman of the City Plan Commission, and advertising executive William C. D'Arcy advanced the proposal for a riverfront memorial to Jefferson during the early years of the Great Depression, subsequently enlisting the support of Democratic Mayor Bernard F. Dickmann. These advocates conceived of the memorial as an effective means of eliminating the blighted riverfront district as well as creating jobs to reduce the burden of public relief. Writing in support of their proposal, the St. Louis *Globe-Democrat* editorialized:

We have seen a patch of civic ugliness grow from the levee westward until it embraced many blocks of a once-thriving downtown district. As the blight has eaten its way in three directions from the waterfront, it has become increasingly apparent that something must be done and at the same time restore the area to its rightful place in the civic scheme. The Jefferson Memorial project supplied this very impetus. (9 June 1937)

Local civic leaders, speaking on behalf of additional funds for the Memorial project before Congress in 1950, also recalled its Depression origins:

The improvement of the area had been considered and discussed for two generations before PWA came into existence in 1933. In the beginning the discussion was from the angle of getting rid of the eyesore presented by the old dilapidated buildings on the riverfront.
    Then in 1933 came PWA and, as the St. Louis newspapers pointed out, the thought of this great Historic Memorial on the site of "Old St. Louis" fitted aptly into the then new pattern of PWA and the opportunity so presented was sought to be availed of. ("Record of Reports" 18)

Intensive lobbying efforts by a wide spectrum of Memorial supporters finally resulted in passage of a joint resolution of the United States Congress in June, 1934 creating the United States Territorial Expansion Memorial Commission. Although the Jefferson National Expansion Memorial was subsequently deemed ineligible for Public Works Administration funding, St. Louis Mayor Dickmann persuaded New Deal officials of the political necessity for the Roosevelt administration to support improvements on the St. Louis riverfront.[9]

Not everyone shared the enthusiasm of the St. Louis contingent for the project, however. A February 23, 1936 article in *The Nation* severely criticized the project as a political boondoggle. According to *The Nation*:

The project's sponsors proposed to sell back to the government at $325,000 an acre land that the government had bought in 1803 for four cents an acre and sold to settlers at $1.25. (Ward, P. 267)

The Memorial project was subsequently shifted to the National Parks Service under the auspices of the Historic Sites Act, which allowed the federal government to acquire historic sites as national landmarks. President Roosevelt signed legislation on December 22, 1935 designating the area as the first national historic site.

The first historical area to come under the provision of the Historic Sites Act was an enigma from the beginning. The first section of the Historic Sites Act of 1935 reads as follows:

It is hereby declared that it is a national policy to preserve for public use historic sites, buildings and objects of national significance for the inspiration and benefit of the people of the United States. (666-668)

However, the Jefferson National expansion Memorial was by no means a traditional historic preservation project such as the Vieux Carre historical district established on the New Orleans riverfront during the 1930s. In the opinion of Charles Hosmer, Jr., one of the founders of the historic preservation movement in the United States, "It was an urban renewal project with a veneer of history used to coat an expenditure for unemployment relief" (626). National Park Service officials who came to St. Louis to work on the project quickly learned that local officials and leaders had little or no interest in preserving the architecture of old St. Louis, despite the fact that the Memorial district contained one of the finest ensembles of cast-iron architecture in the country.[10] Charles

Peterson, founder of the Historic American Buildings Survey which surveyed the historic riverfront buildings, remarked that "Mr. [Luther Ely] Smith wanted them down and what Mr. Smith wanted, he got" (McGrath 15).

In 1935 a hotly-contested city bond issue to provide funds for clearing the old riverfront district won the necessary two-thirds majority vote, despite widespread claims of voting irregularities and fraud. Recalling the controversial bond issue, St. Louis historian James Neal Primm noted that opponents of the bond issue for the Memorial "had a strong case, but the judge, impressed by the importance of the project or perhaps by its powerful sponsors, refused to kill the memorial" (Primm 481). Protracted lawsuits by forty-three property owners, mostly small businesses, postponed demolition for four years. By October 9, 1939 when Mayor Dickmann removed the first brick from the memorial district, the sense of urgency for the project had considerably diminished. The St. Louis *Post-Dispatch* reported the event in the back sections of the newspaper, while news of war in Europe dominated the front page (Hamler 128).

Not everyone shared the prevailing image of the old riverfront as a threat to decent society. The riverfront had historically harbored diverse ethnic groups, from eighteenth-century French fur traders and mulatto slaves to figures like the ill-fated lovers Frankie and Johnny. To the very end of its existence, the riverfront district remained a noisy, disorderly place populated by "outsiders." One local journalist of the St. Louis *Globe-Democrat* recalled the last days of the old riverfront:

There was merriment and nostalgia at the Rock House with its cherrywood bar on the first floor and night club on the second; there was Harry Turner's Blue Lantern, there was Little Bohemia run by artist Savo Radulovic, which served beer on candle-lighted tables with checkered cloths, and where customers played chess or talked away the night to the somber lilt of gypsy or Slavic music. (*Sunday Magazine* 24 Sept. 1961)

Building sacrifices historically represented a symbolic imitation of the primordial sacrifice that originally gave birth to the world. Viewed in this context, the razing of the historic St. Louis riverfront

Demolition of historic riverfront buildings. Photograph courtesy of the Jefferson National Expansion Memorial/National Park Service.

for the Jefferson National Expansion Memorial can be regarded as a rejection of actual American urban history in favor of a more attractive setting consistent with the urban form preferred by progressive civic leaders.[11]

Symbolic forms have traditionally been the visible supports of society and major sources of cultural cohesion. As the early years of the Depression revealed, the loss of traditional symbols creates uncertainty, and with uncertainty comes disequilibrium. The sight of bread lines, bonus marches, homeless families and farm disclosures were difficult images for most Americans to comprehend. The Japanese surprise bombing of Pearl Harbor in 1941 represented yet another shock to the self-image of the slowly-recovering nation.

Although World War II delayed the construction of the Jefferson National Expansion Memorial, it also altered and deepened its cultural significance. Americans sought to give meaning and form to the unprecedented cultural experiences that had unfolded since 1929. For example, Aaron Copland's dramatic "Fanfare for the Common Man" imbued the war effort of a mass society with a heightened sense of nobility. In the words of Mr. Justice Felix Frankfurter:

The ultimate foundation of a free society is the binding tie of cohesive sentiment. Such a sentiment is fostered by all those agencies of the mind and spirit which may serve to gather up the traditions of a people, transmit them from generation to generation, and thereby create that continuity of a treasured common life which constitutes a civilization. We live by symbols. (Mead 141)

When Luther Ely Smith, chairman of the Jefferson National Expansion Memorial Association, met with National Park Service director Newton Drury in 1944, he expressed his personal opinion that there should be one central feature, a single shaft, a building, an arch, or something else that would symbolize American culture and civilization. He wanted something "transcending in spiritual and aesthetic values" which would attract people from other nations to the Memorial (JNEMA Papers 4 Nov. 1944). The program for the design competition of the Memorial in 1948 stated a similar sentiment:

The Architectural Memorial is to be conceived as a striking element, not only to be seen at a distance in the landscape but also as a notable structure to be remembered and commented on as one of the conspicuous monuments of the country. (Jury of Award 1)

However, the design competition for the Jefferson National Expansion Memorial also reflected the historic concerns of progressive civic leaders about the economic viability of the downtown commercial district. Advertising executive William D'Arcy wrote:

We shall create and build not only a national memorial of great beauty; we shall rebuild a great part of the economic value of our city, which has suffered from years of neglect. (JNEMA Files 3)

Progressive Architecture magazine commented:

Local interest in the competition...has centered on a solution for the memorial site that will revitalize the riverfront and also provide a parking area or areas to serve the nearby shopping and financial district of the city. ("Progress Report" 18)

The fundamental difference between national and local interests was clearly revealed in the design competition instructions about the main purpose and function of the Memorial. One section of the design competition instructions concentrated on commercial benefits to the region, while the other focused on the historical significance of the Memorial to the nation as a whole.

The winning design in the 1947-48 Memorial competition embodied a masterful resolution of these competing interests. Many of the nation's leading architects submitted entries for the prestigious $40,000 first prize in this national design competition. Nevertheless, the jury voted unanimously and with considerable enthusiasm on the very first ballot for Design No. 44. One journal report of the Competition noted:

The other competitors were prompt and vocal in their praise. It was easier to lose first place when the winner had so obviously been inspired. ("Jefferson Memorial" 92)

The Jury of Award selected Entry No. 44, a large stainless steel arch sited within a dense forest on the riverfront. It remarked that the design "tends to have the inevitable quality of a right solution" (Jury of Award 3). William W. Wurster, dean of the School of Architecture and Planning at Massachusetts Institute of Technology and chairman of the Jury of Award, told the New York *Times* that "the design's principal feature, a stainless steel arch 590 feet high, was in the same class as the Washington Monument" (19 Feb. 1948), while the *Times*' architectural critic wrote approvingly of "a slum area made into a gracious park" (Louchheim). A new cultural symbol had been fashioned for post-war American society that realized the traditional image of the city.

Source: Box 18, Memorial Competition Drawings. Photograph courtesy of the Jefferson National Expansion Memorial/National Park Service.

Chapter IV
Monument to the Dream

I was trying to reach for an absolutely permanent form—a high form.

Eero Saarinen

There was an ironic, significant incident involving the Jury of Award's selection of the winning design for the Jefferson National Expansion Memorial. The Jury quickly sent a congratulatory telegram to the architectural office of Saarinen & Saarinen, Associates of Bloomfield Hills, Michigan to notify the winner of his selection. Not surprisingly, the secretary addressed the telegram to the famous Finnish-American architect and urban designer Eliel Saarinen, who headed the prestigious firm and had submitted an entry to the competition. Members of the staff broke out champagne, and the entire firm, including Eliel's son and partner Eero, joined in toasting his great success. It was not until three days later that the mistake was corrected and Eero learned that his own futuristic design had actually won first prize.[1] It would not be the last irony surrounding "one of the most puzzling projects in American history" (Hosmer 626).

The incident of mistaken identity provides valuable insights into the life and career of architect Eero Saarinen. The Memorial competition represented his first victory in a major design competition as well as a significant departure from his previous work. It also signified the growing rift within the Saarinen architectural firm between Eero's progressive architectural vision and the dominant historicism of his renowned father Eliel. On an even deeper level, the Jefferson National Expansion Memorial symbolizes the life-long search of Eero Saarinen to create an ideal

65

form of architecture that would harmonize nature and technology for an increasingly fragmented modern age. Saarinen believed that:

Architecture is much more than its utilitarian meaning—to provide shelter for man's activities on earth. It is certainly that, but I believe it has a much more fundamental role to play for man, almost a religious one. (*Saarinen on his work* 5)[2]

Saarinen intended the Jefferson National Expansion Memorial as a monument to Thomas Jefferson, the American nation, and to the modern age. He regarded the "spirit" and the "function" of the Memorial as inseparable entities, and labored mightily to create a work that would be "all one thing" (Temko, *Eero* 18). His work on the Memorial typified his lifelong struggle to establish his own identity as an architect and to give meaningful form to the rapid technological advances of post-war American society. Architectural critic Rupert Spade perceived in its design an appropriate testament to its creator:

Here in a way Saarinen's quest both began and ended; the first major design to separate him from the work of his father...and one of the last to be completed after his own death, the Jefferson Memorial expresses both the ambition and the emptiness of the architect's meteoric career. (Spade 19)[3]

The story of the Memorial's design demonstrates the role of individual genius in giving shape to cultural ideals. Saarinen contended that "great architecture is always informed by one man's thinking" (*Saarinen on his work* 10). Eero Saarinen embodied the struggle of modern architects to comprehend and to cope with increasingly sophisticated technologies. In the form of the Jefferson National Expansion Memorial, the life history of its designer became inseparable from that of the larger society in which it took shape. As psychoanalyst Erik Erikson concluded, "We cannot separate life history from history" (13).[4]

Psychohistory provides a valuable conceptual model for understanding Saarinen's lifelong search for an ideal architectural form. Psychohistory involves the interdisciplinary study of individual and collective life utilizing the combined methods of psychoanalysis and history. It seeks to clarify understanding of the

personal aims of significant historical figures in relation to their
historical and generational contexts. Psychohistory requires
considerable awareness of the early lives of historical figures, as
well as close attention to their unconscious motivations. It
supplements, rather than replaces, conventional biography by
highlighting lifelong tendencies or concerns of these individuals.
As the incident involving the mistaken identity in the Memorial
competition suggests, psychohistory offers a particularly resonant
approach to understanding the creator of what one critic termed
"the most audacious national monument attempted in the twentieth
century" (Temko, *Eero* 10). Saarinen himself observed:

My father, Eliel Saarinen, was a fine architect and a leader in his generation...I
shall be grateful if my efforts are as successful. If they are, I would prefer to be
recognized for my own success. (*Saarinen on his work* 14)

Erikson has successfully applied the methods of psychohistory
to an analysis of Thomas Jefferson's efforts at establishing a new
American cultural identity. Erikson defines a sense of identity to
mean:

A sense of being at one with oneself as one grows and develops; and it means,
at the same time, a sense of affinity with a community's sense of being at one
with its future as well as its history—or mythology. (27)

By examining how Jefferson's lifelong concerns such as
architecture and agriculture relate to their developmental context,
Erikson demonstrates how his significant creations grew out of
personal struggles that intertwined with the public events of the
American Revolution and the founding of the Republic.
Generational matters of inheritances, rebellion and education
preoccupied Thomas Jefferson. "The earth belongs in *usufruct*,"
he wrote to Madison, "always to the living generation" (qtd. in
Soucie 218). For example, Jefferson objectified his political theory
of a natural aristocracy, derived from his socially-mobile father Peter
and his aristocratic mother's refined tastes, in creations such as
Monticello and the University of Virginia. His plantation at
Monticello provided a living laboratory for agricultural,

vinticultural and horticultural experiments. In his own hand-
written epitaph he cited the Declaration of Independence, the
Virginia Statute of Religious Freedom and the University of Virginia
as his patrimony. In creations such as these he attempted to give
institutional expression and a sense of order to an emerging
American sensibility of individual freedom.

The methods of psychohistory that Erikson utilized in his
analysis of Thomas Jefferson prove equally fruitful when applied
to the architect of his memorial. Generational matters also concerned
Eero Saarinen deeply. He once wrote:

The only architecture which interests me is architecture as a fine art. That is what
I want to pursue. I hope that some of my buildings will have lasting truths. I
admit frankly I would like a place in architectural history. (*Saarinen on his work*
14)

Saarinen attempted to achieve this sense of identity and
continuity in his design for the Jefferson National Expansion
Memorial. Discussing his early attempts to conceptualize his
Memorial design, Saarinen recalled the many discussions after the
Second World War about national war memorials:

I felt that monuments like the Lincoln and Washington monuments served their
real purpose in reminding us of the great past, which is so important in relation
to looking toward the future. ("Saarinen Tells")

Like Jefferson with his beloved Palladio, Saarinen attempted
to integrate the influences of powerful predecessors into his own
creations. The deep influence of his formidable father remained
with Eero Saarinen throughout his career. Eliel Saarinen "was a
man very unlike Eero, alternately stern and sparkling" (McQuade
107). The elder Saarinen, himself the son of a Finnish Lutheran
minister, regarded spiritual values as inseparable from practical
ones. He even wrote a book on architectural design theory in which
he described civilized life itself as a "search for form."[5] Echoing
his father's ideas, Eero himself later reflected that:

A better name for architect is form-giver and until his death in 1950, when I started
to create my own form, I worked within the form of my father. (*Saarinen on his
work* 14)

The values and architecture of Frank Lloyd Wright also exerted
a deep and lasting influence upon Eero Saarinen. To Saarinen,
Wright symbolized "the Michelangelo who saw the building whole,
as one organism, and...saw that organism in relation to its
surroundings" (Temko, *Eero* 34). Saarinen believed that at its best,
Wright's architecture always harmonized with nature. It was "all
one thing," as Eero Saarinen wished his own work to become.
"Sometime Frank Lloyd Wright will be re-evaluated," wrote
Saarinen, "and his great concept of architecture where everything
is all one organism, all one thing, will be appreciated" (*Saarinen
on his work* 13).

These two influences, classicism and organic architecture,
helped give form to his winning design for the Jefferson National
Expansion Memorial. Saarinen's original intent had been to create
a great domed structure similar to the Jefferson Memorial sited
in the nation's capital. Before he conducted a site visit to the St.
Louis riverfront, Saarinen had envisioned an open-vaulted structure,
possibly a "Pantheon in lacework," because of the historic
associations of the dome form with Thomas Jefferson. "We began
to imagine some kind of a dome which was more open than the
Jefferson Memorial in Washington," Saarinen recalled. "Maybe it
could be a great pierced concrete dome that touched the ground
on just three points" ("Saarinen Tells How"). However, he rejected
the dome form because it would not rise up from the levee in an
inspiring fashion. Saarinen was looking for an ideal form
appropriate to the physical setting of the St. Louis riverfront. Only
after creating numerous models using his ever-present pipe cleaners
as structural elements did he settle upon the form of a triumphal
arch.[6]

However, the triumphal arch represented only one element of
a much larger whole. A Japanese architectural critic, particularly
impressed with Saarinen's ability to relate architecture to its physical
setting, commented:

I think that Saarinen always had this foremost while designing, the great harmonization to the surrounding environment at which he was so successful. In particular, he was successful at the Saint Louis Arch. (Pelli 224)

According to Saarinen's final design for the landscape of the Memorial, the Arch would soar up from within a mighty forest. "We believed that what downtown Saint Louis most needed was a tree-covered park," Saarinen said. "We wanted to have the most nature possible toward the city" (qtd. in Wood). Aline Louchheim, the New York *Times* architectural critic who later became Saarinen's second wife, reported:

The Saarinen plan envisages that most of the area will be so densely covered with trees that it will be a forest-like park, a green retreat from the tension of the downtown city. (Louchheim)

The roots of this design principle also extend deeply into Saarinen's background. His father Eliel once wrote:

It must be borne in mind that the family and its home are the cornerstones of society, and that man's physical and mental development depend largely upon the character of the environment in which he is nurtured as a child, where he spends his manhood, and where he does his work. (*The City* 1)

Eero Saarinen spent most of his life in rural or suburban surroundings. From his childhood at the Saarinen's family home in Finland to his education at the suburban Cranbrook Academy near Detroit through his collegiate years at Yale University, Saarinen matured among carefully planned and organized landscapes. Even after achieving international stature, he lived in a remodeled century-old farmhouse close to Cranbrook while working at his architectural office in the Detroit suburb of Birmingham, Michigan. Saarinen shared Thomas Jefferson's passion for harmony with nature in both his life and architecture.[7]

His family's home of granite and timber eighteen miles outside of Helsinki, Finland was named Hvittrask after the magnificent lake it overlooked from a wooded bluff. Eliel Saarinen had fled the capital city of Helsinki along with some like-minded colleagues to create a 38-room rural retreat. Despite its pastoral setting, Eliel endowed Hvittrask with every modern convenience. Hvittrask evolved into a famous artists' colony, frequented by the likes of Jean Sibelius, Maxim Gorki, Gustav Mahler and the Swedish sculptor Carl Milles. It proferred an extremely fertile setting for an idealistic and creative young architect like Eero Saarinen.[8]

Eero—the Finnish name for Eric—was born into this idyllic setting on August 20, 1910. Both highly sensitive yet extremely energetic as a child, he was also a prodigy capable of sketching with either hand. His father imparted a strong work ethic to Eero, as well as the moral resolution the Finns call *sisu*. *Sisu* consists of the capacity to go beyond the limits of resources and physical energy. *Sisu* requires deep personal commitment to any creative endeavor, and it became one of Eero's guiding principles. In a requiem written shortly after Saarinen's untimely death, one biographer reported:

Personal memoirs of Saarinen by friends center on his unswerving force, his quiet confidence in methodical work to produce inspiration, and his lust for that work. He did not approach a problem in design or in life and walk around it, observing. He threshed it, like wheat. (McQuade 103)

At the age of twelve Eero won first place in a Swedish matchstick design contest. That same year Eliel won second prize in the international design competition for the Chicago *Tribune* tower. Aware of the new opportunities America afforded an architect, in April 1923 Eliel moved his family from their idyllic Hvittrask retreat to the United States. The experience was both jarring and portentous. On Eero's first night in Manhattan, he told his father, "The traffic is all mixed up and wrong. It ought to be changed" (Temko, *Eero* 14)

Eliel soon acquired a powerful patron in Detroit auto executive George Booth, who commissioned him to develop a fine arts academy in suburban Bloomfield Heights, Michigan. Eero received much of his education at this Cranbrook School, an elegantly landscaped and ordered environment principally designed by his father. All the fine arts were integrated into the Cranbrook curriculum. It became, in effect, an Americanized version of the Saarinen family home at Hvittrask, a center of high culture and environmental awareness. Except for Frank Lloyd Wright's colony at Taliesin, it was the only place of its kind in the heart of America (Temko *Eero* 14).

Not surprisingly in light of his upbringing, Saarinen employed the university campus model for his design for the Jefferson National Expansion Memorial. "Universities are the oases of our desert-like civilization," he asserted. "They are the only beautiful, respectable pedestrian places left" (*Saarinen on his work* 11). Saarinen shared the vision that prompted Thomas Jefferson to call the University of Virginia "an academic village," embodying the finest expression of organic *civitas*.[9] Together with his father, Eero worked on many campus planning projects throughout the United States such as Drake University, MIT, Concordia Senior College in Indiana and at his *alma mater*, Yale University. "We can learn from the experience of a university," he concluded, "which in a sense is a permanent environment, whereas so much of the American city is not" (qtd. in Temko, "Something Between" 82). [10]

At Stiles College of Yale University Saarinen successfully met what he called "the challenge of building proud buildings of our own time that are in harmony with the outdoor space and the existing buildings of other times" (*Saarinen on his work* 12). Working among buildings from several generations, Saarinen blended new construction materials and technology harmoniously into the historic university setting. One architectural critic noted that Saarinen:

Retained the best...of Yale architectural attributes, the small, intricate outdoor spaces among the buildings. The characteristic of the architect which the Yale Colleges bring out is probably the one Eero Saarinen himself was the proudest of in his office: "Responsibility to the client and to the surroundings." (McQuade 117)

He also applied these principles to the design of the Jefferson National Expansion Memorial. As Saarinen elaborated and refined the Memorial design, he attempted to create an increasingly campus-like environment. He repeated the curve of the arch form in paths and walls surrounding the Arch itself, and also suggested them in reflecting pools on the ground. The terrain was sculpted and reshaped into a gently rolling landscape. "The idea of using related curves in landscaping and surface design of the Memorial," he reflected, "came to me as a kind of principle that would give a classic unity to the whole conception" (qtd. in Dunlap 12). All of the lines within the site of the Memorial, including the paths and roads, even the railroad tunnels, were "brought into the same family of curves to which the great arch itself belongs" (*Saarinen on his work* 18).

This classic unity that Saarinen sought to achieve in the Memorial and in all his work was the organic expression of *civitas* that he found disappearing in modern civilization with the exception of the university campus. Schooled in city planning and urban design by his father, Eero Saarinen became deeply concerned about the destruction of *civitas* in modern civilization. As his early comment about Manhattan traffic indicated, the chaotic appearance of most American cities appalled Saarinen. His father taught Eero that each object should be regarded in its next largest context— a chair in a room, a room in a house, a house in an environment, the environment within a city plan (Temko, *Eero* 14). Saarinen later observed:

We should stop thinking of our individual buildings. We should take the advice my father gave me, "Always look at the next larger thing." When the problem is a building, we should look at the spaces and relationships that that building creates with others....In the process (the architect) will gradually form strong convictions about outdoor space—the beauty of the space between the buildings— and if he does, he will carry his conviction on to his most important challenge— how to build cities. (Temko, *Eero* 26)

Saarinen applied this principle, with characteristic *sisu*, to the Jefferson National Expansion Memorial. He involved himself not just with the design of the Memorial but also attempted to deal with its larger context. "One cannot think of the Park alone," he remarked. "The Park, the City, the west side of the Mississippi and the east side—these are all parts of one composition" (JNEMA files 2 Oct. 1957). "The other side of the river...must be brought into the whole composition," he emphasized. "We must make this a great, green park" (*Saarinen on his work* 18).

The surrounding and future downtown buildings framing the Memorial particularly concerned Saarinen. He argued that it must be seen in a proper context:

Excessively high buildings will hurt the memorial. The limit of what is good for the memorial is about 200 feet. Such a height provides a very good relationship with the memorial, making the arch about three times higher than the buildings. ("Saarinen Feels" 7)[11]

His concern was to prevent construction of high office towers that would compete with the Memorial or dwarf the historic Old Court House, which was also a part of the Memorial landscape.

Local civic leaders did not all share Saarinen's viewpoint. They had historically regarded the Memorial as a stimulus to downtown redevelopment, and quickly rejected height limitations for the area immediately surrounding the Memorial. One architectural journal editorialized:

Strangely and deplorably silent were the voices of the powerful inner circle of Saint Louis business and civic leaders, who in recent years have helped the city earn a reputation for fostering music and other cultural activities. In this instance the city was turning its back on architecture and completely rejecting its responsibility as a national trustee charged with developing the area around the national memorial arch and park in a complementary manner. ("Saarinen Feels" 7)

Although Eero shared many elements of his father's traditional views about urban design, he increasingly moved away from Eliel's architectural theories. Eero had originally intended to become a sculptor, and had studied for a year at the Grand Chaumiere in Paris. After a year he abandoned that pursuit to undertake formal architectural training in the Beaux-Arts classicism of the Yale University School of Architecture. After graduating with honors in 1934, he spent the next two years studying European architecture on a travelling fellowship. Gothic architecture and the cityscapes of Europe left an indelible impression upon his imagination.

During the late 1930s and early 1940s, Eero's work began to evolve in a new direction. His father's architecture was deeply steeped in humanism rather than technology, looking more to the past than to the future. Eero rejected the nineteenth-century Arts and Crafts aesthetic that characterized Cranbrook in favor of industrial design and a machine aesthetic more characteristic of the new generation of modern architects. He attempted to achieve a more streamlined, functionalist architecture than his father's monumentalist style.[12]

After his work for the OSS during World War II, Eero assumed increasing responsibility from his aging father within their firm. The Saarinen architectural firm was heavily engaged at that time in campus planning projects, as well as developing a monumental civic center scheme along the Detroit riverfront and a war memorial in Milwaukee. Their design for the new General Motors Technical Center in Warren, Michigan, reveals the increasing tension between two architectural visions. The progressive International Style of many of the curtain-wall buildings designed by Eero is juxtaposed with an immense lake and a water tower, clear evidences of Eliel's continuing influence.

Eero's winning design for the Jefferson National Expansion Memorial represented a dramatic break from the dominance of his father, as well as a breakthrough for modern architecture. Aline Louchheim, who later became Saarinen's second wife, observed:

It has a simplicity which should guarantee timelessness; yet the audacious engineering, the material, and the implications of science make it wholly contemporary. It seems, indeed, an aesthetic transformation of such functional creations as bridges and dams in which, to date, modern architecture has achieved its greatest perfection. ("Modern Monument")

The Jefferson National Expansion Memorial embodies many of the basic assumptions of modern architecture. Saarinen rejected the traditional dominance of Beaux-Arts classicism. Instead, Saarinen argued in the New York *Herald Tribune* that he had "tried to think of the simplest forms, based on the natural laws of mathematics" (26 Feb. 1948). He shared Jefferson's and Ead's faith in the "self-evident truths" of a reasonable and orderly universe that would reveal their true nature to the patient observer through logic and science. He attempted to comprehend the world "as it really is," rather than rely upon traditional forms.[13]

Despite his reputation as a modern architect, however, Saarinen simply did not fit into any definitive architectural style. Each project or building seemed to require an original solution, an ideal form. He once remarked:

I feel strongly that modern architecture is in danger of falling into a mold too quickly—too rigid a mold. What once was a great hope for a great new period of architecture has somehow become an automatic application of the same formula everywhere. I feel, therefore, a certain responsibility to examine problems with the specific enthusiasm of bringing out of the particular problem the particular solution. (*Saarinen on his work* 6)

Saarinen therefore moved toward the modern systems approach in his architecture. This procedure involved conducting a detailed analysis of a design problem with the help of innumerable sketches. Its goal was to find a unique architectural form and structure for each problem. Mock-ups and modeling techniques, which have become standard architectural practices since the Second World War, owe a great deal to Eero Saarinen. He employed models not only to demonstrate the design but to help determine it, while mock-ups were full-scale sections of buildings designed to test the effects of the latest technical advances. For example, part of the monumental stairway of the Memorial was built in full-size mock-up form to evaluate its dramatic effects.

Until his untimely death from brain cancer in 1961, Saarinen attempted to give meaningful form to the chaotic world of modern technology. His innovative designs for modern airports demonstrate this ambitious objective. His design of poured concrete for the TWA terminal at New York's Idlewild Airport resembled the giant form of a swooping bird. Dulles Airport at Chantilly, Virginia is widely regarded as one of his most important creations. Along with the sweeping shape of the terminal of this first airport exclusively intended for jet aircraft, Saarinen created the mobile passenger terminals that would allow greater efficiency in loading and unloading the mammoth aircrafts. As one critic observed:

He tried to overtake the fast-moving train of technology...and impose upon it a system of checks and balances similar in effect to the discipline of classical and Renaissance architecture. (Spade 9)

The Jefferson National Expansion Memorial epitomized Saarinen's quest to overtake technology. Just as Thomas Jefferson gave significant form to his new vision of America, Saarinen, too, had to devise a new form to realize Jefferson's memorial. Although arches have historically been utilized in monumental architecture, what Saarinen did was to liberate the arch form from the physical restraints of older masonry materials such as brick and stone. The form had traditionally been regarded as a strength caused by two weaknesses, the legs of the arch supporting one another. However, the height of Saarinen's Arch created unprecedented stresses that would cause it to snap in high winds. By joining an inner frame of carbon steel with a surface of stainless steel, Saarinen created a single dynamic structure from one end to another that was all one thing.

Jefferson had once remarked about architecture:

When buildings are of durable materials, every new edifice is an actual and permanent acquisition to the state, adding to its value as well as to its ornament (qtd in Fitch 55)

Saarinen shared this Jeffersonian idealism regarding architecture. He chose stainless steel for the Memorial because it "would seem to be the most permanent of the materials we have...the thing one could trust most" (Temko, *Eero* 19). The basic shape of the Arch was then carefully studied and compared with various historic structures in terms of proportions. Allan Temko reported:

As the work went ahead in 1958, he drew upon his experience with curving forms at MIT, the Yale hockey rink, and TWA, seeking a faultless arch form, contemplating the monumental arches of the past, and the vaults and buttresses of Gothic cathedrals....He wished this arch to rise up in a single, aspiring movement. (*Eero* 122)

The Jefferson National Expansion Memorial epitomized Saarinen's quest to overtake modern technology. This unprecedented marvel of modern engineering drew heavily upon advanced aerospace technologies. One trade journal commented:

The Arch is also, in effect, a testament to modern man's pioneering accomplishments. It stands as shining proof of the engineering and material developments that have brought man to his newest and farthest frontier—space. (American Iron and Steel Institute)

The MacDonald Construction Company, builder of the Arch, was one of the fifty largest construction companies in the United States. It had made its reputation building defense installations during the 1950s, such as Nike sites in Alaska and Titan missile launching facilities in the state of Washington. MacDonald used the computers of McDonnell Aircraft Corporation in St. Louis to prepare a "critical path" construction schedule. This method, similar to that later employed in the space program, identified and controlled every step of the labyrinthine construction process (Terry, "Big Builder's" 3D).

The Arch was constructed with a stainless steel outer shell very similar to the design of jet aircraft fusillages, in which the stressed outer surface carries the structural load. The 312 tons of thrust in the structure's triangular, hollow legs had to be jacked apart by a steel spreader in order to insert the final section at the peak. Once that task was completed, the two legs became one seamless structure. The same thrust that threatened to pull down the two legs then kept the structure stable in winds up to 155 miles per hour. The unprecedented architectural problems posed by the Jefferson National Expansion Memorial make it a prototype of Saarinen's romance with technology. One architectural critic concluded:

It is very much of its time, kind of a great structural gesture showing off the technological structural abilities. I think it's one of the best things that's ever been done. (Venturi 220)

There are, however, certain ironies involved in using a prototype of modern architecture to celebrate the significance of the frontier in American life. For example, many of the steelworkers on the project memorializing America's westward expansion were Mohawk Indians, renowned for their ability to work fearlessly and well at incredible heights (Riley 14). Although Eero Saarinen stood squarely in the architectural tradition of the individual genius like Jefferson, James Eads, or Frank Lloyd Wright, construction of the Jefferson National Expansion Memorial testified to the dominant influence of the modern, post-war corporation. Construction of the Jefferson National Expansion Memorial reveals the ironic conclusion of Eero Saarinen's dream, a fitting counterpoint to its enigmatic origins. In Rupert Spade's words:

It is after all a simple arch, a form known to the ancients and associated with architecture for some thousands of years; but it is also a hollow-frame structure, engineered with considerable skill and daring. More like a circulatory system than a skeleton, it is crammed with unseen movement. Seen from a distance the simple form is deceptive; inside is the seething technology of a new world, waiting to get out. (19)

Each day in the auditorium beneath the Arch, hundreds of visitors view a technically superb film entitled *Monument to the Dream*, sponsored by the American Iron and Steel Institute. The film, replete with breathtaking shots from high above the arch, celebrates the miracles of technology and the extraordinary teamwork of the construction workers and engineers who constructed the Arch. Rather than a return to frontier self-sufficiency, the Jefferson National Expansion Memorial represented progress into an increasingly complex and interdependent New Frontier.[14]

Chapter V
The New Frontier

Show me your city, and I will tell you what are the cultural aims of its population.
Eliel Saarinen, *The City*

Eero Saarinen did not live to see his dream realized. Construction of the Jefferson National Expansion Memorial was delayed throughout the 1950s, as the city of St. Louis and federal agencies haggled with local railroad companies about relocating the elevated railroad tracks which ran through the Memorial grounds. Saarinen died from brain cancer in 1961, just as excavation of the foundations for the Memorial was commencing.[1]

President John F. Kennedy authorized the final funds needed for construction of the Memorial in 1962. Like Saarinen, he, too, did not live to see the completion of the modern memorial to the ethos of the frontier. Nevertheless, his effective advocacy of a New Frontier spirit seems especially appropriate to the spirit of Saarinen's daring architectural form and landscape design. Far more than merely a memorial, the Jefferson National Expansion Memorial is a prototypical American landscape that, like Thomas Jefferson's "invention" of America, participates in our myths even as its own image continues to evolve. It effectively symbolizes the New Frontier of a post-industrial American society.

Since the days of Thomas Jefferson, the American Dream has always been predicated upon the progressive transformation of traditional concepts into new forms of experience. In the words of cultural historian Daniel Boorstin:

81

A new civilization found new ways of holding men together—less and less by creed or belief, by tradition or by place, more and more by common effort and common experience, by the apparatus of daily life, by their ways of thinking about themselves. (*The Americans* 2)

Boorstin raised some troubling questions in the early 1960s about the fundamental values of this new American society that was taking shape. He contended that the insatiable American desire for new experience was creating impossible new levels of expectations and leading to unrealistic demands upon natural resources.[2] He compared the eighteenth-century world views of Founding Fathers like Jefferson to those of the late twentieth century. The major difference, Boorstin argued, was that images had replaced ideals as the major element holding American society together. While the ideals of the founders of the Republic had functioned as claims upon their lives that demanded service to a cause, an image, on the other hand:

Is something we have a claim on. It must serve our purposes. Images are means. If a corporation's image of itself or a man's image of himself is not useful, it is discarded. Another may fit better. The image is made to order, tailored to us. (*The Image* 198

The form of a people's architecture provides important clues to their cultural values. Thus it was appropriate that the church spire of the Old Cathedral dominated the skyline of early St. Louis, while the towering form of the Arch dominates its contemporary horizon.[3] The subsequent uses of the Jefferson National Expansion Memorial since its construction help reveal the transformation into such an image-conscious American consumer society.

The official dedication of the Jefferson National Expansion Memorial crystallized the long-standing tension that existed between two opposing conceptions of its historic purpose. In a speech presented at the dedication ceremony of the Memorial on May 25, 1968, Vice-President Hubert H. Humphrey declared that "from now on, St. Louis' Arch is America's magnificent monument." However, the Superintendent of the Memorial did not share the Vice-President's sanguine perspective and idealism. He had warned that:

It would be unfortunate, if through some misunderstanding of its purpose, the Gateway Arch were to be considered as simply an attractively designed backdrop to the Saint Louis riverfront. (McCue 13G)

The relentless American pursuit of Progress has subsequently realized the Superintendent's warning. Like the use of the Jeffersonian gridiron system of land development for real estate speculation instead of the orderly development of a yeoman republic of small farmers, this tension between national ideals and local boosterism had characterized the Memorial plan from its inception. "The Arch," observed St. Louis historian James Neal Primm, "was the symbol of progress in St. Louis, as was evident from the eagerness of business to be associated with it" (484).[4] As the Arch neared completion, one national magazine editorialized:

This $32 million project, costing nearly $5 million more than the Louisiana Territory itself, is noteworthy, too, as an illustration of how government planning can go awry. The memorial was conceived in 1933 and among other things was designed as a four-year economic pump-priming project to stimulate business and increase employment. (James 8)

During the 1930s National Park Service professional historians planning to supervise and research a project within the Historic Sites Act of 1935 found themselves administering an enormous demolition and renewal program. The Second World War did not eliminate this tension, either. Eager to regain the project momentum lost during the Second World War, in 1950 St. Louis sent a delegation of local civic leaders to lobby Congress for funds to implement the winning design of the 1947-48 design competition. Testimony in 1950 by local civic leaders to a Congressional subcommittee on appropriations clearly reveals their commercial focus for the project. They consistently cited the Memorial project as a development catalyst rather than a memorial to the ideals of Thomas Jefferson or America's historical experience. For example, the Chairman of the St. Louis Real Estate Board's Committee on Commercial Development stated:

The development of this site would rejuvenate the entire downtown district....It unquestionably would attract national attention and bring untold profits to the entire city of Saint Louis and the federal government....It would...provide a monument to our city that will give us national recognition throughout the years. (JNEMA, *Record of Reports* 22)

Dollar investments and real estate values, rather than curatorship of the land, were typically cited as the project's rationale. "Establishing this area as a national park created substantial values," observed one speaker, "which will be realized as the memorial is developed" (*Record of Reports* 21). In particular, the speakers praised the Memorial for its potential as a tourist attraction for an increasingly mobile automobile-oriented society. The President of the St. Louis Chamber of Commerce noted:

All the necessary conditions are present for adding this all-important area to the splendid array of feature tourist attractions. It is both good business and constructive national policy to proceed....The Jefferson National Expansion Memorial is a perfectly sound business venture. (*Record of Reports* 58)

The possibility that a conflict might exist or even arise between local business objectives and national interests was never mentioned during the testimony.

The Jefferson National Expansion Memorial has played a major role since its construction in all three dimensions cited by civic leaders in their testimony. It has been an important factor in downtown redevelopment efforts, tourism, and as a symbol of St. Louis. Its evolution during the past twenty years parallels the transformation of America into the New Frontier of a post-industrial society.

The Jefferson National Expansion Memorial quickly helped stimulate a dramatic transformation of downtown St. Louis. "Besides commemorating the westward trek of the American pioneers," commented a national journal, "it [the Memorial] marks the Saint Louis Bicentennial of 1964" (Jensen 65). As he launched the Bicentennial of St. Louis on February 14, 1964, President Lyndon Johnson characterized the efforts of the city to renew itself in the following words:

As the Gateway to the West, Saint Louis became one of the finest and most important cities of the world. But at the very summit of her glory, the blight that was to deface dozens of American cities also struck St. Louis. The incredible vitality of this proud queen of Mid-America began to erode. . . .

You faced a hard choice and you made it. The people of Saint Louis chose progress—not decay. A new spirit of Saint Louis was born. And today, you look forward to the future with new pride and confidence. (Jordan 606)

The Jefferson National Expansion Memorial became the focal point of the city's renewal efforts. The St. Louis *Globe-Democrat* proudly proclaimed that "our Arch is more than the most magnificent attraction of Saint Louis; it is part cause, part symbol, and focal point of the renascence [sic] of this city" (29 Oct. 1965).

National observers echoed this civic boosterism. One commentator observed:

Now taking shape on the Mississippi riverfront in Saint Louis is America's newest and highest national monument—a majestic arch of gleaming stainless steel. It will inevitably come to symbolize Saint Louis. (Hicks 169)

National Geographic devoted a cover story to the city's urban renewal efforts, citing the Gateway Arch as the foremost example of the rebirth of St. Louis (Jordan 605-641). *Time* magazine reported on the close relationship between construction of the Memorial and downtown redevelopment efforts as an example of progressive city planning that would reverse the decline of central cities:

Saint Louis is proudly watching the 630-foot high Gateway Arch, designed by the late Eero Saarinen as a symbol of westward expansion, rise where shabby warehouses once lined the Mississippi. Foundations in the foreground are for 28-story apartments, serviced by new expressways and designed to bring scattered residents back to the area where the city began. (6 Nov. 1964)

However, even as architects and city planners talked about urban renewal and downtown revitalization more than ever before, cities in their traditional forms as concentrations of people and institutions were rapidly melting into the sprawling suburban landscape.

Aerial view of arch and downtown facing northwest.

To understand American cities, one must relate them to the larger political economy and culture of the nation. Major social shifts have radically altered the form and economic functions of central cities like St. Louis since World War Two. Interstate highways, federally subsidized mortgage loan programs and urban renewal programs reduced housing opportunities in central cities while encouraging people to live in surrounding regions. Central cities increasingly became the corporate headquarters for a post-industrial service economy and housing of the last resort for those left behind by the swift social and economic changes.[5]

Urban geographers often characterize the most recent stage of American economic development as a "transactional society." In this highly mobile society, information rather than goods is processed, advertised and distributed. These transactions mainly occur in a number of regional command and control centers such as San Francisco, Houston, Atlanta and Boston.[6] High-level managerial functions, key information institutions, the delivery of services from hospitals to high-class boutiques and specialized leisure areas typically characterize these new centers. Others, like St. Louis, vie for a competitive share of the new growth industries.

However, the internal needs of corporations and other organizations competing in a world economy now tend to supersede external factors such as geographic position or labor supply in determining location decisions. Unlike the geographic determinism proclaimed by James Eads and civic boosters during the nineteenth century, a constantly shifting society based upon rapid transfers of information and capital is increasingly being substituted for traditional towns and cities predicated upon pools of raw materials and unskilled labor. Stimulated by advanced technologies such as microelectronics and telecommunications, a rapidly changing economic system driven by organizations whose size and international scope place them above local political control now imposes its own abstract logic of strategic decisions over the traditional approach of place-based activities, cultures and politics.

Nevertheless, these new patterns have not developed in a historical vacuum. Like a palimpsest, they are created on the forms of the preceding levels of urbanization. They connect networks that are both functionally useful and socially valued. Cities still form the contexts in which cultures and societies are produced and transformed, just as cities like St. Louis are themselves produced and transformed by those societies and cultures.

Cities still function as conservators of cultural symbols associated with both the experiences of the past as well as future aspirations, and these symbols help condition human perceptions of their spatial order.[7] The Jefferson National Expansion Memorial is just such a potent symbol. It provided the spatial context for the transformation of downtown St. Louis into a major corporate headquarters. According to the President of Downtown St. Louis, Inc.:

The Arch was extremely important....It was a major investment in the 1960s, following decades of disinvestment. It was the first real investment since the 1920s. (Lombard, "Gateway Arch" 11)

One local journalist called the redevelopment of downtown St. Louis "the greatest (boom) in the downtown area in more than a half-century" (Hannon). Downtown St. Louis, Inc., the district's business organization, calculated that the total reinvestment in the downtown area from 1958 until 1982 totaled over $1.25 billion (Lombard, "Gateway Arch" 11).

The Memorial did not merely generate a building boom; it gave it direction and form. "Without the Arch, the revitalization of downtown would not have happened," said Art Baebler, executive vice-president of the Regional Commerce and Growth Association. "Before the Arch, the central business district of downtown was up on Tucker Boulevard." "Every building right up Market Street [the major east-west thoroughfare] came as a result of the Arch," said Alfred Fleishman, chairman emeritus of the advertising firm of Fleishman-Hilliard, Inc. "Before the Arch it was all just winos and bums" (Lombard, "Gateway Arch" 11). The construction of major office towers for banking, insurance and telecommunications corporations along Market Street proceeding west from the Memorial clearly reflects the major structural changes in American society.

Evolving functions for the historic downtowns have also affected their surrounding neighborhoods. The advanced corporate services required by the new patterns of production and rapid informational demands require different types of workers from traditional urban manufacturing jobs. According to Baebler of the Regional Commerce and Growth Association:

The work population of downtown may not have changed that much in absolute numbers since before the Arch, but the old textile jobs on Washington Avenue have been replaced by more sophisticated workers.... The Arch has been the reason for the rise in quality of jobs, and for the fact that the number of jobs has been maintained at all. (Lombard, "Gateway Arch" 11)

These structural economic shifts have stimulated not only downtown areas but also housing demands by these new workers. Not surprisingly, St. Louis has also become one of the leading cities in the country in terms of housing rehabilitation to accommodate these types of information workers.

The Jefferson National Expansion Memorial was not only important to the city as a catalyst for downtown development. In the words of local historian James Neal Primm:

The theme and purpose of the Memorial had been magnificently realized. As a result, Saint Louis became one of the world's major tourist centers. (Primm 484)

Tourism and leisure activities comprise major growth industries in post-industrial American society. Tourism combines production and consumption into one place, in which places themselves become objects for consumption. Instead of their traditional activities such as mass merchandising, textile shops and shoe manufacturing, downtowns like St. Louis now provide riverfront tourism, specialized shopping, historic districts and cultural activities for a new leisure class. "The nature of the Arch is important," noted the President of Downtown St. Louis, Inc. "It's a major visitor attraction, the foundation for the visitor industry downtown. All of the hotels downtown are there because of the Arch. They all try to get as close to the Arch as possible" (Lombard, "Gateway Arch" 11).

One journalist called the Arch "a new Mecca for American tourists" (Hicks 170), while another reported:

Developers...are hoping the memorial's Gateway Arch will prove to be a second Eiffel Tower...drawing enough visitors to ensure the success of their ventures. (James 8)

The St. Louis Convention and Visitors Bureau reported that over 50 million people had visited the Jefferson National Expansion Memorial since 1967. By 1974 the Jefferson National Expansion Memorial was listed as the fourth-most visited human-made attraction, following Lenin's Tomb and two Walt Disney theme parks. The United States Travel Service reported it to be one of the top seven world attractions. Rather than a rainbow, the Memorial proved to be the pot of gold.[8]

The ability of the Memorial to compete for visitors with Disney theme parks suggests that is has been increasingly assimilated into an image-conscious consumer society. In fact, civic leaders immediately solicited Walt Disney to build a major entertainment center near the Arch upon its completion. As at Disney theme parks, visitors to the Memorial:

come to admire a memorial—half shrine to commemorate the past, half dream to inspire the future. (Riley 14)

The Gateway symbolism of the Jefferson National Expansion Memorial seems especially appropriate to the fluidity of a post-industrial society. Highly mobile Americans in a post-industrial society have become much less conscious of the identity of their cities than were ancient, medieval, or Renaissance citizens. A modern city is a "sphinx without a secret," in a state of constant informational excitement (Bogdanovic 144). A "transactional society" constantly uses up its symbols in the process of generating and meeting new demands. This process has been occurring to the Jefferson National Expansion Memorial. For example, the manager of the Marriott Pavilion Hotel in downtown St. Louis noted that "all of our advertisements have a picture of the Arch. It's a major,

major backdrop to the hotel" (Lombard, "Gateway Arch" 11). The Superintendent of the Memorial recently commented that the Arch is now much less important as a catalyst for urban redevelopment than as an image for the city.

Religious symbols such as icons traditionally connoted fixity and permanence; they remained far beyond the demands of ordinary existence. The symbols of contemporary American life, on the other hand, deal with the flux and impermanence created by the shifting demands of a consumer society.[9] For example, the 1980 St. Louis telephone directory listed seventeen Arch business firms, from the Arch Bootery to the Archview Cafeteria, an Archable real estate firm, a plain old Archco, an Archland Dome and forty-nine Archway companies including a funeral home, a massage parlor and a brokerage house. There was also a Big Arch leasing firm and 131 Gateway enterprises, including a bartending school, a Bible fellowship, a loan company, a bank, an Oriental herb store and a corkball club (Primm 484). "An urban park is going to have this problem," said Superintendent of the Memorial Jerry Schober:

Certain groups would like to exploit it, like a business venture that someone feels will complement the purpose of the park just perfectly, when you know they just want to line their pockets. Most people want to use the park rather than preserve it. (Lombard, "Schober" 5)

The National Park Service quickly discovered the need for guidelines concerning the use of the Memorial in advertising or other reproductions. "Because the Gateway Arch is a National Memorial equal in dignity and grandeur to other great memorials and is becoming a symbol of St. Louis," it said, "it should be utilized in advertising, displays, cartoons, etc., with restraint" (U.S. Dept. of the Interior, *Use of Photographic*). Restraint, however, has seldom characterized local attitudes toward the Jefferson National Expansion Memorial. Boorstin regarded the lack of restraint as a fundamental American problem stemming from the overblown expectations that the new consumer society created. He remarked:

Never have people been more the masters of their environment. Yet never has a people felt more deceived and disappointed. For never has a people expected so much more than the world could offer. (Boorstin, *The Image* 4)

The mastery of the environment achieved by post-industrial American society creates other dilemmas of appreciation as well. The concept of a national park at the heart of a major metropolitan area poses a true American anomoly. Although the national parks owe much more to the Romantic movement of the nineteenth century than to Jeffersonian agrarianism, they too share Jefferson's belief in nature as a source of moral rather than commercial values. Their goal is preservation rather than development of the land.[10] The Superintendent of the Memorial clearly articulated this preservation ethic:

The park is for the benefit and enjoyment of the public and future generations. . . . You can't use up the resource just as it is, you've got to save it so that your kids can enjoy it in the same way. (qtd. in Lombard, "Schober" 5)

However, the Memorial also signifies a major urban renewal effort by St. Louis civic leaders to compete more effectively within post-industrial American society. These progressive boosters had consistently emphasized economic redevelopment rather than preservation; the riverfront land was to be developed for profitable new uses. In many respects, this view appears far more representative of basic American values. The ideology of progress and newness constitutes the core of the American myth.

Observers of American culture since the 1960s have increasingly been raising questions about these traditional myths and about the meaning of our historic experiences for new, post-industrial conditions. Traditional beliefs about America's mission, the dominance of WASP cultural groups and the costs of progress in relation to the natural environment have all been seriously challenged. Boorstin, for example, criticized what he regarded as an accelerating American tendency to ignore the discipline of history in favor of superficial, transitory images created by advertising for immediate advantages such as profit or political success. As a corollary concern, he also warned against what he termed the pseudo-event, an ambiguous creation of unclear origins designed to satisfy the burgeoning American appetite for new experiences, without reference to any historical validation. "What the image is in the world of value," wrote Boorstin, "the pseudo-event is in the world of fact. It is synthetic, believable, passive, vivid, simplified, and ambiguous" (Boorstin, *The Image* 185).

The mammoth VP Fair held on the Memorial grounds during the Fourth of July weekend crystallizes the tension between alternative views of the Memorial and provides a clear example of a pseudo-event that threatens the symbolic significance of this unique cultural resource. Like most American Fourth of July celebrations it is a festival of abundance, billed as "America's biggest birthday celebration," annually consuming a million cups of beer and hundreds of thousands of hot dogs. Unintentionally echoing Boorstin's critique, one local reporter characterized the fair as "a ball and a bash, hoopla and hullabaloo. It's 1764 and 1878 and 1904 and 1981 meshed into three days; a memory of the past, a born-again yesterday, the first Veiled Prophet parade and the World's Fair repackaged for the space age" (Kimbrough, "VP Fair" 5). The VP Fair's relationship to the American historic experience of westward expansion symbolized by the Arch is ambiguous and inauthentic.

Its origins and purposes are also deliberately ambiguous. Organizers call the VP Fair "a throwback to the organization's festivals a hundred years ago and an effort to boost civic pride and the city's image" (Plott).[11] The three-day celebration descends from a local harvest celebration that originated in the 1870s. Like Eads Bridge and the Louisiana Purchase Exposition, the original Fair presented a progressive image of St. Louis to the world. The original organizer of the Veiled Prophet parade, Alonzo Slayback, remarked back in 1878:

The thing I like best about it is that for the next year and the year after and so on for the next hundred years, the strangers who visit our...Fairs can be entertained by the second, third, or one hundredth panorama of progress by the same mysterious brotherhood. (Kimbrough 8)

1986 VP Fair. Photograph by Kurt Hosna.

That "mysterious brotherhood" Slayback mentioned refers to the Veiled Prophet Organization, a highly selective and secretive social institution that originated during the Gilded Age. The VP Organization includes the upper echelons of St. Louis businessmen as its members. One reporter noted:

Several key participants in the planning of the fair, who requested anonymity, said a riverfront fair was planned to serve a two-fold purpose. First and foremost, it would boost the image of the city and, secondly, it would hopefully bring the Veiled Prophet organization back to the type of prominence it enjoyed prior to the 1960s. (Smith, B. 1E)

The VP Fair thus uses the Memorial not as an artifact to provide for a balanced assessment of the historic experience of westward expansion, but as a sign system to support the existing social relations in the community.

Pseudo-events like the VP Fair are not new in the American experience, but they significantly differ in numbers, scale and technical sophistication from their antecedents. More importantly, pseudo-events such as the VP have become not just a form of civic boosterism, but an indispensable component of a consumer-driven economy. National media exposure resulting from the 1976 Bicentennial celebration under the Arch encouraged civic leaders to institutionalize the event in the form of the VP Fair. In the intense competition between cities and states for tourist dollars, such publicity is vital.[12] A pseudo-event such as the VP Fair enables a city like St. Louis to obtain a decided advantage in this life-or-death competition to influence the flow of tourists and capital. The VP Fair now attracts national media coverage ranging from the *National Geographic* to the "Today" show.

Not surprisingly, the Gateway Arch figures quite prominently in this scenario. "Since the Saint Louis image is centered on the Arch," wrote one reporter, "it made sense to use the monument and grounds for...promotion" (Vogel-Franzi 52). While entertaining at the 1982 VP Fair, comedian Bob Hope glanced up at the Arch and quipped, "It looks like a MacDonald's with a gland condition" (Ross "2 Million" 1A). Hope's comment, perhaps unintentionally, clarifies the relationship of the VP Fair to the

Jefferson National Expansion Memorial: arches, whether golden or stainless steel, promote the product.

However, the Fair's emphasis upon size and spectacle places enormous stresses upon National Park Service staff and the carefully cultivated grounds of the Saarinen landscape. "The purpose of the fair is not consistent with the design of the park," facilities manager Bob Kelly stated. "The Arch is designed for the people, it is not designed as a fairground" (Ross, "VP Fair" 1A). Tramping crowds and sudden thundershowers reduced the grounds to a muddy swamp in 1982, while trucks driving along the pedestrian walkways severely damaged more than fifty trees of the emerging forest that Saarinen had envisioned for the site. The VP Fair organization eventually picked up the cost of the repairs. "It is good business," said VP Fair director Charles Wallace (Ross, "VP Fair" 1A). The long-term impacts of the VP Fair on the fragile Memorial grounds, however, remain uncertain.

Using the Memorial to capture media attention poses another fundamental challenge to the National Park Service's curatorial approach to the Memorial. Park officials had steadfastly resisted daredevil activities at the Arch, despite requests by VP Fair officials and others, as inappropriate to its lofty national purposes. Nevertheless, others assign totally different meanings to the Arch. Hollywood stuntman Dan Koko, who held the world free-fall record, said the Arch is ideal for one of his well publicized jumps. "It's such a dynamic structure," he said. "It makes me real eager."[13] As Boorstin had predicted, such eagerness for new experience in post-industrial America would recognize no boundaries. In November, 1980, a skydiver named Kenneth W. Swyers parachuted onto the top of the Arch, while his wife and friends filmed the event for a television show. His parachute collapsed upon impact, and he slid down the north leg of the Arch to his death.

If architecture has to concentrate its efforts on symbolizing a way of life and the public realm, then it encounters difficulties when those elements lose their credibility.[14] Like America itself, the Memorial has become the stage for a variety show that accepts no guidelines, knows no limits. In the New Frontier of post-industrial society symbolized by the Jefferson National Expansion

Memorial, Americans were no longer held together by ideals but "by countless gossamer webs knitted together by the trivia of their lives" (Boorstin, *The Americans* 148).

Epilogue
Genius Loci

Americans have always subscribed to Eden, and proceeded to transform it in the process.

Alan Trachtenberg, *Brooklyn Bridge: Fact and Symbol*

The view from the top of the Gateway Arch, our tallest national monument, clearly reveals the polarities of the American myth of progress. From an elevation of 630 feet a visitor can gaze for miles in the directions of east and west. To the west one perceives the city transformed into a romantic landscape, a new form of American nature. Roland Barthes' description of the Eiffel Tower applies with equal accuracy to the soaring Gateway Arch:

[It] makes the city into a kind of nature; it constitutes the swarming of men into a landscape, It adds to the frequently grim urban myth a romantic dimension, a harmony, a mitigation.... (Barthes 8)

To the east one sees the barren wasteland of the East St. Louis riverfront; its abandoned railroad yards, its billowing chemical factories, its crumbling neighborhoods; the people whom Progress has left behind. The visitor quickly abandons this view in favor of the more pleasant prospect. The disparity depicted from atop our largest national monument constitutes the root problem of American culture. We have lost sight of Eero Saarinen's holistic vision of American society in which all elements participate in the transformation of nature.

Just as an arch achieves stability by balancing the tensions between the legs, a culture is defined as much by its tensions as by its consensus values.[1] Such tensions provide the necessary tensile strength to keep the culture alive and dynamic, but these tensions may also generate upheaval and may even bring about complete

99

cultural collapse. Cultural historian Michael Kammen has suggested an interesting analogy between our ideal physical and cultural forms:

America historically has achieved the ultimate stability of an arch (think of the Natural Bridge in Virginia, beloved by Jefferson): Those very forces which are logically calculated to drag stones to the ground actually provide props of support—derived from a principle in which thrust and counter-thrust become means of counterpoise. (297)

American culture has historically achieved its celebrated political stability and minimized class conflicts by emphasizing individual prosperity in an abundant future to be created by technological advances. The Jefferson National Expansion Memorial objectifies this cultural ideal of American Progress refined and civilized within a green, forest setting, where every aspect of nature appears new and open to discovery. The view is quintessentially American. In the words of James Oliver Robertson:

The Americans are a Chosen People, part of a new plan for Creation, specially endowed by their Creator as representatives of the possibilities and potentialities of the Brave New World. They are on the cutting edge of history, pathfinding, discovering, and settling the chaotic wilderness which is just beyond—over the next hill, across the next desert, over the next ocean, on the next satellite or planet. (122)

Despite recent setbacks to American self-esteem dating back to the Vietnam conflict, these cultural assumptions remain very much alive in contemporary American society. Speaking at the commemoration of the 25th anniversary of the National Air and Space Administration (NASA), President Reagan remarked:

What you've proven with the success [of the space shuttle] is that there is never a time when we can stop moving forward, when we can stop dreaming. (qtd. in Grey 40)

Doorways, arches and other types of openings traditionally symbolized the tension between old and new ways of life. The Gateway Arch, a symbolic opening to the West, triumphantly celebrates our endless American pursuit of happiness and new experience while discarding the shackles of Old World traditions. Americans have traditionally defined themselves and their society in terms of mobility in pursuit of abundance. Most Americans were brought up to believe in mobility, that elusive pursuit of happiness beyond the next frontier. The Jefferson National Expansion Memorial perfectly captures this American ethos.

As insightful observers of American life have frequently noticed, for nearly two centuries the expanded American middle class has believed and acted upon the cultural assumption that the meaning of life involved the acquisition of ever-increasing social status, income and authority flowing out of a limitless wilderness.[2] Having overthrown traditional social restraints as vestiges of the Old World, Americans sought to create the *Novus Ordo Seclorum* that the back of our dollar bills proudly proclaim. Material abundance and continual growth would guarantee genuine individual freedom and social stability. Despite lingering doubts and growing evidence to the contrary, we have tenaciously clung to the notion that poverty and inequality would be eliminated by continually expanding economic abundance. That dream has animated Americans like Thomas Jefferson since the origins of the American Republic: most of us were nurtured upon that same dream. We cannot easily disavow that premise of our culture, even though it contradicts the other dream Americans have also harbored since the founding of the Republic—that of living in a commonwealth, the harmonious yeoman Republic envisioned by Thomas Jefferson.[3]

No human society, not even the yeoman Republic championed by Thomas Jefferson, has been able to foresee the hidden path leading from the steady introduction of new technologies controlled and administered by an increasingly unaccountable elite to the destruction of core values that give life meaning and depth. The Hamiltonian program has undermined and eroded the Jeffersonian ideals. Just as increasing dependence upon trade with the white settlers undermined native American cultures, so the self-sufficient Republic of yeoman farmers envisioned by Jefferson was subverted by eagerly embracing the benefits of Progress. The hardships of the Oregon Trail and the promises of Madison Avenue represent alternative gateways to human fulfillment.

Caught between these two tendencies, Americans have been and remain deeply divided about the meaning of their historical experience. It is not surprising, therefore, that the Jefferson National Expansion Memorial, which symbolizes both the frontier experience and the romance of technological progress, is our largest national monument. By celebrating a symbol of the frontier past, we can express our nostalgia for a more open, "natural" society of rugged individualism amid a wilderness setting. On the other hand, by celebrating the unprecedented achievements of corporate technology in the "Monument to the Dream," as the Gateway Arch has been christened, we can also interpret American history in terms of technological and material progress. We want to have it both ways; the duality of the Jefferson National Expansion Memorial satisfies our mythic needs.

To perceive the utopian aspects in the American dream of Progress and material abundance, however, does not necessarily commit one to the path itself. We do not have to accept all of its implications, nor even agree that it can only be achieved within this particular economic and social framework, in order to share the dream. From Jefferson through the Southern Agrarians and continuing today, other myths about the American land have sought a hearing in our cultural dialogue. Mainstream American culture has historically assumed that as long as economic growth continued, the private sector could and would resolve our remaining social issues. Each new technology would ensure that the future would be even more abundant. Now that our traditional ecological image of a limitless frontier has been so seriously polluted that we can no longer assume continually rising living standards, we are beginning to understand that the validity and survival of the American Dream require far more than exclusive devotion to material progress.[4] The steamboat, the railroad, the automobile, the airplane and even the space shuttle have not overtaken the elusive ideal of Happiness.

As he marveled at turn-of-the-century international expositions like the 1904 Louisiana Purchase Exposition in St. Louis, where the concept of a riverfront memorial to Thomas Jefferson originated, American historian Henry Adams formulated a critical question for modern industrial America: would the new Republic represent any values other than sheer size and continual growth? What had happened, Adams wondered, to the original concept of the Republic created by Founding Fathers such as his great-grandfather? The Jefferson National Expansion Memorial poses the same troubling question for contemporary Americans that perplexed Henry Adams. One could easily apply the words of cultural historian Daniel Boorstin, so similar to Adams' reflections at the 1904 World's Fair, to the thoughts of a visitor gazing skyward at our largest national monument disappearing into clouds overhead:

Now the American assignment seemed to come no longer from the conscious choices of individual citizens, but from the scale and velocity of the national projects themselves. Growth, ever more and faster, seemed to have become the nation's whole purpose.

Man's problem of self-determination was more baffling than ever. For the very power of the most democratized nation on earth had led its citizens to feel inconsequential before the forces they had unleashed. (*The Americans* 558)

Continuing cultural vitality depends upon questioning cultural symbols in relation to changing historical circumstances. A continuous process of pruning, of adapting to a future that requires new forms of expression, is a necessary function within every society. We need to step outside the myths of American history in order to utilize the insights made available to us through other stories or traditions. A fuller understanding of the Jefferson National Expansion Memorial and, by extension, the possibilities for American society, depends upon this critical step in awareness. As a character in Thomas Pynchon's novel *Gravity's Rainbow* concluded, "Somewhere, among the wastes of the world, is the key that will bring us back, restore us to our earth and to our Freedom" (525). We need some alternative views of rainbows.

Like Nick Carraway, the narrator in F. Scott Fitzgerald's *The Great Gatsby*, we need to achieve a deeper understanding of the myths that propel us toward "the orgiastic future" depicted by the Jefferson National Expansion Memorial. There is indeed something "gorgeous" about this simple yet complex national monument, with its aura of limitless possibilities and its hidden technological underpinnings, that compels the imagination. Mirroring Jay Gatsby's "platonic conception of himself," architect Eero Saarinen's idealized form reveals our own deep-rooted desire to overcome and transcend history. Somewhere Gatsby had "killed a man"; the Memorial, too, required the sacrifice of a sometimes sordid yet real history in the form of forty blocks of old riverfront buildings to create an idealized landscape. On the gently rolling grounds of the Jefferson National Expansion Memorial, one can actually experience Nick Carraway's vision of the "inessential houses" melting away and the "fresh, green breast of the New World" reappearing. As one Jefferson National Expansion Memorial brochure describes the scene:

The Memorial as you see it now is an inspiring sight. The gleaming Gateway Arch, the majestic Old Courthouse, the two river outlooks, the railroad blending gracefully into its riverfront surroundings—these represent the flowering of a magnificent dream. (*Official Brochure* 2)

As the other side of the view from atop the Arch indicates, however, in reality we have continually failed to create the idealized communities symbolized by our arches. In their place we have often left a valley of ashes. We have tried to explain away these increasing social contradictions by projecting their ultimate resolution into the abundant future to be created by technology. Not even the final closing of the frontier could destroy this American cultural idea. "It eluded us then," Fitzgerald concluded," "but that's no matter—tomorrow we will run faster, stretch out our arms farther, and one fine morning..." (182).

Despite its utopian qualities, the American Dream of progress is not the complete answer to human aspirations. The question of the future is not what is the new man, the American, but what we can become in the future without denying our connections to the collective human experience. Cultural symbols like the Jefferson National Expansion Memorial have historically appealed to humanity's need for true *genius loci*, that sense of knowing one's place in the order of the cosmos. Although Jefferson believed the use of the fruit always belonged to the living generation, the land itself belonged to "the hundredth and thousandth generation." In his Memorial we need to celebrate not simply Jefferson's belief in Progress, but also recall his fundamental respect for the world of nature and its cultivation as the proper basis for an enduring culture.

Mainstream American culture has traditionally ignored this responsibility to preserve the land for future generations. Certain aspects of Eastern and native American traditions contain far more wisdom in this respect than our linear view of progress into an infinitely expanding future. Like a sacred mountain, the Gateway Arch also recalls the archetypal dome of heaven. In 1980 the St. Louis Art Museum commissioned noted fashion photographer Joel Meyerowitz to create a photographic essay of the Gateway Arch. After observing it from literally hundreds of angles, Meyerowitz found himself captivated not only by its visual qualities but by its *genius loci*, the spirit of place it so powerfully communicated to him. "It is my Mount Fuji," he wrote, "a presence that feeds me" (qtd. in Duffy 5). Unfortunately, our never-ending pursuit of the ever-receding green light of happiness has ignored such traditional precepts concerning humanity's place in the cosmos. Mastery rather than mystery has characterized American attitudes toward wilderness and nature.

Perhaps we can derive new meaning for our archetypal national monument from cultural traditions that American Progress has buried beneath its surge toward the future. For example, anthropologist Gregory Bateson has suggested that although the totemism of primitive peoples in certain respects was incorrect, it nevertheless revealed a deeper truth of enduring value for modern society. According to Bateson, totems provided clues to the systemic quality of the larger Creation to which we are inextricably linked. The rainbow described in the Old Testament story of Noah and the Ark, symbolizing a new union between Nature and Culture, represents such a totem. In Bateson's words:

The natural world around us really has this general systemic structure and therefore is an appropriate source of metaphor to enable man to understand himself in his social organization. (484)

Such a totemic understanding of American culture suggests that we cannot indefinitely postpone the consequences of an increasingly wasteful consumer society. God, as Bateson reminds us, is not mocked; the rainbow symbolized a threat of the fire next time as well as a promise of a new order.

Perhaps a new and fuller vision of the American Land can be created with elements of such a totemic understanding.[5] Beneath the Jefferson National Expansion Memorial, beneath even the historic riverfront that was razed for the Memorial, lay ancient Indian burial mounds. The last surviving mound was leveled in the 1860s to make way for the progress represented by James Eads' railroad bridge, just as the old riverfront and railroad trestle later gave way for the Gateway Arch. Like many native American cultures, these ancient burial mounds were sacrificed to American Progress. Yet they, too, are part of the *genius loci* of the Jefferson National Expansion Memorial. The words of a Lakota Sioux prayer, applied to the Jefferson National Expansion Memorial, represent the missing but vital dimension of our American myth:

Guide us in our days; help each of us as your Children to be proud of our Great Heritage, to know and to be who we are, and to share with others, becoming one humanity within your everlasting love, as the many colours come together to form the rainbow in the sky. (*Oxford Book of Prayers* 74)

View of Gateway Arch from Canokia Mounds. Photograph by Kurt Hosna.

Notes

Prologue

[1]See also Gene Wise's article "Paradigm Dramas in American Studies," *American Quarterly*, 31 (Bibliography issue, 1979) 293-337 for an analysis of the role of what Wise termed "examplars" such as Miller and Vernon Louis Parrington in shaping American culture studies during different historical periods.

Introduction

[1]I am particularly indebted to Richard Zaner's *The Way of Phenomenology: Criticism as a Philosophical Discipline* (Indianapolis: The Bobbs-Merrill Company, 1970) for my understanding of a phenomenological approach to the study of culture. For another example of the phenomenological method applied to the study of culture, see Peter Berger and Thomas Luckmann, *The Social Construction of Reality: A Treatise in the Sociology of Knowledge* (New York: Anchor Books, 1966).

[2]See Edward Relph, *Place and Placelessness* (London: Pion Limited, 1976) preface.

[3]See Mircea Eliade, *The Sacred and the Profane*, trans. Willard R. Trask (New York: Harcourt, Brace & World, 1959). Another excellent work in this field is Erich Isaac, "Religion, Landscape, and Space." *Landscape* (Winter, 1959-60) 14-18.

[4]Among the many excellent works in the burgeoning field of cultural geography, particularly helpful works included: Grady Clay, *Close-Up: How to Read the American City* (Chicago: U of Chicago P, 1973); D.W. Meinig, ed., *The Interpretation of Ordinary Landscapes* (New York: Oxford UP, 1979); Yi-Fu Tuan, *Topophilia: A Study of Environmental Perception, Attitudes and Values* (Englewood Cliffs, NJ: Prentice-Hall, Inc., 1974); and Wilbur Zelinsky, *The Cultural Geography of the United States* (Englewood Cliffs, NJ: Prentice-Hall, Inc., 1973).

[5]See Jay Mechling, "Towards an American Ethnophysics," in *The Study of American Culture/Contemporary Conflicts*, Luther Luedtke, ed. (Deland FL: Everett/Edwards, Inc., 1977) 258.

Chapter I
The Arches of Classical Antiquity

[1]Statement by the Jury of Award on the Winning Design in the Jefferson National Expansion Memorial Competition, Jefferson National Expansion Memorial Archives, 2.

[2]Much of this anecdotal material is derived from an article by Sharon Brown, "Jefferson National Expansion Memorial: The 1947-48 Competition," *Gateway Heritage* 1.3 (Winter 1980) 40-48. This article is a condensation of her Ph.D. dissertation on the administrative history of the Memorial published at St. Louis University in 1982. Dr. Brown provided many valuable insights to this dissertation through both her written works and various conversations we shared. However, any errors or interpretations belong to the author.

[3]See Christian Norberg-Schulz, *Meaning in Western Architecture* (New York: Praeger Publishers, 1974). In addition to the work of Norberg-Schulz, my understanding of architectural symbolism derives from the following works: Charles Jencks, *The Language of Post-Modern Architecture (New York: Rizzoli International Publications, 1984); Sir John Summerson, Heavenly Mansions* (New York: Norton Library, 1963; and Robert Venturi, *Complexity and Contradiction in Architecture* (New York: Museum of Modern Art, 1977).

[4]A particularly useful discussion of early architectural symbols can be found in Siegfried Giedion, "Symbolic Expression in Prehistory and in the First Civilizations," in *Sign, Image, Symbol,* Gyorgy Kepes, ed. (New York: George Braziller, 1966).

[5]The concept of the archetype is derived from the work of Swiss psychologist Carl Jung. See for example Jung, *Man and His Symbols* (Garden City, NY: Doubleday, 1964). Other approaches that I found especially helpful in writing this chapter include: Roland Barthes, *The Eiffel Tower and Other Mythologies,* trans. Richard Howard (New York: Hill and Wang, 1979) and Ernst Cassirer, *The Philosophy of Symbolic Forms* (New Haven: Yale UP, 1957).

[6]Wheatley argues that ancient Chinese and Indian cultures developed symbolic cities to order their habitats based upon "natural" archetypes.

[7]Bateson's thesis, which I share, is that American and Western cultures increasingly viewed humanity outside and above nature. This attitude, coupled with increasingly powerful technologies, has led to contemporary ecological crises. See also Myra Jehlen, "The American Landscape as Totem," *Prospects* 6 (1981) 17-36 for an interesting alternative to the Bateson viewpoint.

[8]Several works contributed to my understanding of the origins and development of early cities. See Edmund Bacon, *The Design of Cities* (New York: Viking, 1967) and Lewis Mumford, *The City in History: Its Origins, Its Transformations, and Its Prospects* (New York: Harcourt, Brace & World, 1961). Mumford's book is widely regarded as one of the definitive works on the history of cities. Many of my concepts on city symbolism were derived from a special issue of *Ekistics* devoted to the topic. See "City Symbols: Sacred and Profane," in *Ekistics: The Problems and Science of Human Settlements* 39.232 (March, 1975), entire issue, Constantinos A. Doxiadis, ed.

[9]For an interesting analysis of the design controversy about height limitations on the surrounding buildings, see "Saarinen feels buildings near Saint Louis national arch should not exceed 200 feet—but city rejects idea," *Architectural Forum* 113. 1 (July, 1960) 7.

[10]See James Marston Fitch, "The Lawn: America's Greatest Architectural Achievement." *American Heritage* 35.4 (June/July 1984) 49-64.

[11]See Rudolph Wittkower, *Palladio and Palladianism* (New York: George Braziller, 1974) for a comprehensive analysis of the architect's work in relation to his historical period.

[12]See also Catherine Albanese, *Sons of the Fathers* (Philadelphia: Temple UP, 1976) for her analysis of the world-view held by the Founding Fathers.

Chapter II
The Gateway to the West

[1]See Perry Miller, *Nature's Nation* (Cambridge: The Belknap Press of Harvard UP, 1967), one of the major studies in this area of intellectual history.

[2]For a thorough analysis of Jefferson's Enlightenment world-view, see Daniel Boorstin, *The Lost World of Thomas Jefferson* (Boston: Beacon, 1948).

[3]See Joseph F. Trimmer, "Monuments and Myths: Three American Arches," 269-77 in *Material Culture Studies in America*, Thomas J. Schlereth, ed. (Nashville, TN: The American Association for State and Local History, 1982). Trimmer compares American attitudes toward nature manifested during several stages of our development, showing the steady process of secularization and loss of awe in the natural world.

[4]Cultural geographer David Sopher regards this view of nature as an American version of what anthropologists have termed *domifuge questing myth*, such as the search for the Holy Grail. Sopher sees many elements of Christian myth transformed into secular American beliefs about nature. See his "Landscape of Home," in *The Interpretation of Ordinary Landscapes*, D.W. Meinig, ed. (New York: Oxford UP, 1979) 129-52.

[5]The definitive work on this subject remains John Reps, *The Making of Urban America: A History of City Planning in the United States* (Princeton, NJ: Princeton UP, 1965).

[6]Catherine Albanese offers an excellent analysis of this tension within American thought; much of this chapter is indebted to her insights. See also Barbara Novak, *Nature and Culture: American Landscape and Painting* (New York: Oxford UP, 1980) for her treatment of this theme in American art and philosophy during the early American Republic.

[7]See Donald F. Dosch, *The Old Courthouse: Americans Build a Forum on the Frontier* (Saint Louis: Jefferson National Expansion Memorial Association, 1979) for an interesting account of the construction of the Court House in relation to city politics.

[8]See also the materials and speeches by Benton in Gwinn Harris Heap, *Central Route to the Pacific* (Glendale, CA: The Arthur H. Clark Co., 1957).

[9]See Chapter 8 of James Neal Primm's *Lion of the Valley: St. Louis, Missouri* (Boulder, CO: Pruett Publishing, 1981) 287-344 for an excellent account of this rivalry.

[10]See the discussion of the modernization process in Stuart N. Eisenstadt, "Studies of Modernization and Sociological Theory," *History and Theory*, 13.3 (1974) 249.

[11]Architectural historian Lawrence Lowic has provided an excellent description of the construction and symbolism of Eads Bridge in his *Architectural Heritage of Saint Louis 1803-1891* (St. Louis: Washington University Gallery of Art, 1982).

[12]See John A. Kouwenhoven, "Eads Bridge: The Celebration," *Bulletin of the Missouri Historical Society*, 30, 3 (April 1974) 159-80. Another excellent treatment of Eads and his work may be found in Joseph Gies, "Mr. Eads Spans the Mississippi," *American Heritage*, 20, 5 (August 1969) 16-21.

[13]See Daniel Boorstin, *The Americans: The Democratic Experience* (New York: Vintage, 1974). See also Ch. 22, "The Myth of the Garden and Turner's Frontier Hypothesis," in Henry Nash Smith's *Virgin Land*, 250-60 for one of the foremost critiques of the Turner hypothesis.

[14]Historian Warren Susman takes considerable notice of the role of international expositions in elucidating cultural values in *Culture as History: The Transformation of American Society in the Twentieth Century* (New York: Pantheon Books, 1984). He specifically cites the Louisiana Purchase Exposition as a valuable but under-studied cultural artifact.

Chapter III
The Image of the City

[1]See Peter J. Schmitt, *Back to Nature: The Arcadian Myth in Urban America* (New York: Oxford UP, 1969) for his discussion of how Progressives created a virtual nature cult during the first two decades of the twentieth century. Schmitt cites such diverse phenomena as Theodore Roosevelt's robust activities, the Boy Scouts and the growth of national parks, among others, to show how an urbanizing American society attempted to use natural images to cope with their new situation. This chapter is heavily indebted to Schmitt's work.

[2]There are many excellent works that deal with this important period. Two that I have relied upon are Howard Chudacoff, *The evolution of American urban society*, 2nd ed. (New York: Prentice-Hall, 1981) and Sam Bass Warner, Jr., *The private city: Philadelphia in three periods of its growth* (Philadelphia: U of Pennsylvania P, 1968).

[3]See Eisenstadt, "Studies in Modernization and Sociological Theory," 228.

[4]The definitive work on this topic remains Morton G. White and Lucia White, *The intellectual versus the city, from Thomas Jefferson to Frank Lloyd Wright* (Cambridge: Harvard UP, 1962).

[5]This represents one of the central themes of Sam Bass Warner, Jr.'s *The Urban Wilderness: a history of the American city* (New York: Harper & Row, 1972), one of the classic works in the field of urban history.

[6]Two works are extremely valuable in understanding this process. For the European experience of city planning, see Carl Schorske, *Fin-de-siecle Vienna: Politics and Culture* (New York: Alfred A. Knopf, 1980), while Robert Wiebe, *The Search for Order, 1877-1920* (New York: Hill & Wang, 1967) examines American

Progressivism as an attempt to create new social and cultural forms appropriate to a largely impersonal industrial order.

[7]See Martin Towey, "Hooverville: Saint Louis had the largest," *Gateway Heritage* 1.2 (Fall 1980) 4-11 for an interesting description of the sociology of these temporary communities on the riverfront. According to Towey, who made extensive use of oral histories to record the views of former residents of the area, there was both a strong sense of commitment to the American Dream and a much higher degree of racial integration in the Hooverville than in the city as a whole.

[8]Two works have been useful in examining this aspect of the Memorial Project. See Richard D. James, "Poky Pump Primer: Saint Louis' Depression Project Nears End—In a Boom," *Wall Street Journal* (June 19, 1964) and April Hamel, "The Jefferson National Expansion Memorial as Work Relief," (Ph.D. dissertation, St. Louis University, 1979).

[9]See the account of the development of the Memorial by National Park Service historian Sharon Brown, "Making a memorial: Developing the Jefferson National Expansion Memorial national historic site 1933-1980," (Ph.D. dissertation: St. Louis University, 1983).

[10]See Siegfried Giedion, *Space, Time and Architecture* (Cambridge: Harvard UP, 1967) 201. According to architectural historian Giedion, "The half-deserted riverfront survived as a witness to one of the most exciting periods in the development of America. Some of its commercial buildings—fur and china warehouses, Pony Express offices, ordinary business blocks—exhibited an architecture far in advance of the ordinary standards at the time of their erection."

[11]Cultural geographer David Lowenthal has discussed the problems of viewing landscapes as history in "Age and Artifact: Dilemmas of Appreciation," *The Interpretation of Ordinary Landscapes*, D.W. Meinig, ed. (New York: Oxford UP, 1979). "The provisional and contingent nature of history is hard to accept," writes Lowenthal," "for it denies the perennial dream of an ordered and stable past."

Chapter IV
Monument to the Dream

[1]See the account in Sharon Brown, "Jefferson National Expansion Memorial: The 1947-48 Competition," *Gateway Heritage* 1.3 (Winter 1980) 40-48.

[2]There are surprisingly few works devoted to this pioneering modern architect who, unlike so many modern architects, wrote very little about his own architecture. His wife Aline compiled this anthology the year following his death to allow the architect's works to speak for themselves.

[3]Spade's perspective on Saarinen's work is more critical than Temko's. Recent articles by post-Modern architectural critics, however, suggest an improving critical opinion of Saarinen's work.

[4]Erikson's analysis of Thomas Jefferson provided much of the theoretical foundation for this chapter on the designer of Jefferson's memorial.

[5]See Eliel Sarrinen, *Search for form: a fundamental approach to art* (New York: Reinhold, 1948).

[6]For a fascinating but technical engineering account of the Memorial design, see "Jefferson Memorial Arch: A Panel," *Building Research—The Journal of the Building Research Institute* 1.5 (Sept.-Oct. 1964) 58-62.

[7]See Chapter 1, "Jefferson and Wright," in James Marston Fitch, *Architecture and the Aesthetics of Plenty* for an analysis of how these two American architects based their designs upon their understanding of a culture grounded in nature.

[8]See Temko's account of Saarinen's childhood in *Eero Saarinen* 10-15.

[9]See James Marston Fitch, "The Lawn: America's Greatest Architectural Achievement," *American Heritage* 35.4 (June/July 1984) 49-64 for a cultural history of the University of Virginia. In 1976 the Jefferson-designed buildings and grounds that comprise the Lawn were judged by the American Institute of Architects to be the single most outstanding achievement of American architecture.

[10]See also Eero Saarinen, "Campus Planning: The Unique World of the University," *Architectural Review* (Nov. 1960).

[11]"Saarinen feels buildings near Saint Louis national arch should not exceed 200 feet—but city rejects idea," *Architectural Forum*, 113.1 (July 1960) 7. See also Eero Saarinen and William Wurster, *Report on the Development of Land Surrounding the Jefferson National Memorial Park* (Saint Louis, 14 Dec. 1948), JNEMA papers, Jefferson National Expansion Memorial Historic Site Archives, St. Louis, Missouri.

[12]See Giedion for his analysis of the powerful influence of Frank Lloyd Wright upon modern European architects while Wright was being virtually shunned in the United States.

[13]See Part I of Charles Jencks' *The Language of Post-Modern Architecture* for his critique of the implicit world-view of Modern architects, a world-view which depended heavily upon technology and science for its rationale instead of being value-free as it claimed.

[14]John William Ward has argued that Americans responded so fervently to Charles Lindbergh because he embodies both their nostalgia for frontier self-sufficiency and their faith in progress through technology. I share Ward's viewpoint, believing that the Jefferson National Expansion Memorial also manifests this American duality. See Ward, "The Meaning of Lindbergh's Flight," *American Quarterly* 10 (Spring 1958) 3-16.

Chapter V
The New Frontier

[1]See Sharon Brown, "The Making of a Memorial: Jefferson National Expansion Memorial 1933-1980," (Ph.D. dissertation, St. Louis University, 1982) for a detailed administrative history of the negotiations involving the railroad tracks.

[2]See Boorstin, *The Image: or, What Happened to the American Dream* (New York: Atheneum, 1962).

[3]See the views of Christopher Tunnard and Henry Hope Reed, *American Skyline: The Growth and Form of our Cities and Towns* (Boston: Houghton Mifflin, 1955) regarding the functions of urban design as cultural symbol.

⁴Primm's work is widely regarded as the most comprehensive history of St. Louis.

⁵Much of the material in this chapter about changing urban functions is derived from Michael Peter Smith, *The City and Social Theory* (Oxford: Basil Blackwell, 1980).

⁶See the analysis in Manuel Castells, "High Technology, Economic Restructuring, and the Urban Regional Process in the United States," *High Technology, Space, and Society*, Manuel Castells, ed. 28, Urban Affairs Annual reviews (Beverly Hills: Sage) 11-40.

⁷See Norman E.P. Pressman, "A planning approach to the study of past urban settlements," *Ekistics* 39.231 (March 1975) 169-71.

⁸See Patricia Corrigan, "The Triumph of the Arch: 1965-1985," St. Louis *Post-Dispatch* 27 Oct. 1965: 13F.

⁹The nature and processes of contemporary image-making are dealt with in *Icons of Popular Culture*. Marshall Fishwick and Ray B. Browne, eds. (Bowling Green, OH: Bowling Green State UP, 1970).

¹⁰The development of the National Park System and the general theme of American attitudes toward wilderness are the focus of Roderick Nash, *Wilderness and the American Mind* (New Haven: Yale UP, 1982).

¹¹For a more scholarly treatment of the history and character of the Veiled Prophet festival, see Karen McCoskey Georing, "Pageantry in St. Louis: The History of the Veiled Prophet Organization," *Gateway Heritage* 4.4 (Spring 1984) 2-16.

¹²One tourism planner reported that somewhere between $3 and $6 billion was spent in 1986 to promote cities and states. See Robert Guskind, "Bringing Madison Avenue to Main Street," *Planning* 53 (1987) 4-11.

¹³See Karen L. Koman, "High Jumper: Hollywood Stuntman Eager to Leap off Gateway Arch," St. Louis *Post-Dispatch* 12 Feb. 1986.

¹⁴See Christopher Jencks, *Language of Post-Modern Architecture* (New York: Rizzoli International) 1984, for an analysis of such difficulties in post-industrial society.

Epilogue: Genius Loci

¹See "Morale and National Character" in Bateson, *Steps to an Ecology of Mind* 88-106.

²This theme is the subject of a classic American Studies work. See David Potter, *People of plenty: economic abundance and the American character* (Chicago: U of Chicago P, 1954). Arguing against Turner, Potter contended that the underlying concept of abundance, rather than simply the frontier, shaped American cultural values. He also shared Boorstin's concern about the function of advertising in creating limitless demands upon natural resources.

³This tension between individualism and the longing for community is the theme of a major analysis of American society and culture by Robert Bellah, et al., *Habits of the Heart* (Berkeley, CA: U of California P, 1985). Bellah and his associates have taken a contemporary view of de Tocqueville's prediction about

the undesirable American tendency to treat oneself as an isolated individual. They conclude that this tendency poses a major threat to American society. This chapter borrows heavily from their analysis of American culture.

⁴See Kenneth Boulding, "The Economics of the Coming Spaceship Earth" *The Environmental Handbook*, Garrett DeBell, ed. (New York: Ballantine Books, 1970) 96-102. Boulding, an economist, suggests that American culture must rethink the assumptions developed during the frontier experience and adopt the cybernetic, systems approach characteristic of the space program in which all actions must be considered in terms of their effects upon the entire system.

⁵See Vine DeLoria, Jr., *The Metaphysics of Modern Existence* (San Francisco: Harper & Row, 1979) for a critique of linear concepts of Progress and what native American world-views could contribute to American culture.

Works Cited

Primary Sources

Government Documents

Architectural Competition for the Jefferson National Expansion Memorial Program, St. Louis, MO, 1947. Jefferson National Expansion Memorial Papers, Jefferson National Expansion Memorial Historic Site Archives, St. Louis, MO.

Bryan, John Albury. Preliminary Draft, Jefferson National Expansion Memorial Administrative History. *Jefferson National Expansion Memorial: Its Origins, Development, and Administration.* Jefferson National Expansion Memorial Association Papers, Jefferson National Expansion Memorial Historic Site Archives, St. Louis, MO.

City Plan Commission. Harland Bartholomew, Engineer. *Plan for the Central Riverfront Saint Louis.* St. Louis, MO, June 1, 1928.

City Plan Commission. Harland Bartholomew, Engineer. *The Problem of Saint Louis.* St. Louis, MO: Nixon-Jones Printing Co., 1917.

Final Report of the Jury of Award to the Professional Adviser on the First and Second Stages of the Jefferson National Expansion Memorial Competition. March 14, 1948. Jefferson National Expansion Memorial Historic Site Archives, St. Louis, MO.

"Historic Sites Act." *United States Statutes at Large.* (P.L. 74-292) 29 Aug. 1935.

United States Department of the Interior, *Outlines of the Jefferson National Expansion Memorial 1933-1945.* St. Louis, MO: 1979. Jefferson National Expansion Memorial Association Papers, Jefferson National Expansion Memorial Historic Site Archives, St. Louis, MO.

U.S. Department of the Interior, National Park Service, Jefferson National Expansion Memorial. *Use of Photographic or Other Reproductions of the Gateway Arch Jefferson National Expansion Memorial* 25 May 1970.

United States Territorial Expansion Memorial Commission. *Reports Approved by the Executive Committee of the United States Commission at its Meeting in St. Louis on April 13, 1935.* Jefferson National Expansion Memorial Association Papers. Jefferson National Expansion Memorial Historic Site Archives, St. Louis, MO.

Other Sources

American Iron and Steel Institute. *The Gateway Arch of the Jefferson National Expansion Memorial.* Jefferson National Expansion Memorial Association files, Jefferson National Expansion Memorial Historic Site Archives, St. Louis, MO.

Architecture and Urbanism. Yoshio Yoshida, Publisher. April, 1984 Extra Edition. Jefferson National Expansion Memorial Association files, Jefferson National Expansion Memorial Historic Site Archives, St. Louis, MO.

Arteaga, Robert F., Arch Construction Photographer. *Building of the Arch.* Jefferson National Expansion Memorial Association files, Jefferson National Expansion Memorial Historic Site Archives, St. Louis, MO.

Brown, Sharon. "Making a memorial: Developing the Jefferson National Expansion Memorial national historic site 1933-1980." Ph.D. dissertation, St. Louis University, 1983.

City Plan Association. *City Plan Association Report.* St. Louis, MO, April 1, 1911.

The Civic League of St. Louis. *A City Plan for Saint Louis: Reports of the Several Committees Appointed by the Executive Board of the Civic League to Draft a City Plan.* St. Louis, MO, 1907.

Civic League of St. Louis. *What the League Is* (What the League Has Done). St. Louis, MO, 1909.

The Eads Bridge. An Exhibition prepared by the Art Museum and the Department of Civil Engineering, Princeton University. Princeton, NJ, 1974.

Hamel, April. "The Jefferson National Expansion Memorial as Work Relief." Ph.D. dissertation, St. Louis University, 1979.

Holt, Glen. "The City's Stainless Steel Rainbow." *VP Fair Magazine.* July 4, 1981, 138-44.

Humphrey, Hubert H. Speech presented at the dedication of the Jefferson National Expansion Memorial, St. Louis, MO. 25 May 1968.

Jefferson National Expansion Memorial Association, St. Louis. *Official Brochure of the Jefferson National Expansion Memorial.* Jefferson National Expansion Memorial Association files. Jefferson National Memorial Historic Site Archives, St. Louis, MO.

Jefferson National Expansion Memorial Association. *Record of Reports to the Committee on House Administration House of Representatives and Hearing Before the Library Subcommittee.* Washington. D.C., May 10, 1950. Jefferson National Expansion Memorial Association Papers, Jefferson National Expansion Memorial Historic Site Archives, St. Louis, MO.

Saarinen, Eero and Wurster, William. *Report on the Development of Land Surrounding the Jefferson National Memorial Park.* St. Louis, MO, Dec. 14, 1948. Jefferson National Expansion Memorial Association Papers, Jefferson National Expansion Memorial Historic Site Archives, St. Louis, MO.

Manuscript Collections
Jefferson National Expansion Memorial National Historic Site Archives.
Jefferson National Expansion Memorial Association files.
Jefferson National Expansion Memorial Association Papers.

National Park Service Papers, 1935-1980.

Papers of Thomas Jefferson, Vols. 1-18. William Boyd, Ed. Princeton, NJ: Princeton UP, 1950.Missouri Historical Society.

James B. Eads Papers.

Luther Ely Smith Papers.

Newspapers and Articles

Daily Missouri *Republican*, 1867, 1887-88.

New York *Herald-Tribune*, 1948.

New York *Times*, 1947-49.

St. Louis *Globe-Democrat*, 1935-86.

St. Louis *Post-Dispatch*, 1933-86.

St. Louis *Star-Times*, 1947-49.

Corrigan, Patricia. "The Triumph of the Arch: 1965-1985." St. Louis *Post-Dispatch* 27 Oct. 1985: 12F.

Dunlap, Robert. "Riverfront Arch Designed to Catch the Eye of the World." St. Louis *Post-Dispatch* 19 Jan. 1958: 12.

Hannon, Robert E. "Keeping Up with the Skyline." St. Louis *Post-Dispatch* 14 Jan. 1969.

James, Richard D. "Poky Pump Primer: St. Louis' Depression Project Nears End—In a Boom." *Wall Street Journal* 19 June 1964: 8.

Kimbrough, Mary. "VP Fair." St. Louis *Globe-Democrat* 20-21 June 1981.

McCue, George. "The Emerging St. Louis Symbol." St. Louis *Post-Dispatch* 10 June 1962: 13G.

McCue, George. "The Emerging Saint Louis Symbol." St. Louis *Post-Dispatch* 10 June 1964: 8.

Plott, Monte. "Army of Volunteers Prepares for Veiled Prophet Festival." St. Louis *Post-Dispatch* 31 May 1981.

Ross, Sandra Bower. "2 Million Jam Riverfront." St. Louis *Globe-Democrat* 5 July 1982.

Ross, Sandra Bower. "VP Fair a Hit with Just About Everyone." St. Louis *Globe-Democrat* 7 July 1982.

Saarinen, Eero. "Saarinen Tells How 'Gateway' was Conceived." St. Louis *Post-Dispatch* 7 March 1948.

Smith, Bill. "The VP Fair is his baby." St. Louis *Globe-Democrat* 27-28 June 1981.

Terry Dickson, "Big Builder's Biggest Challenge—The Arch." St. Louis Post-Dispatch 16 March 1962: 3D.

"Way Back in 1933 Schoolgirl Drew Picture of Arch in Yearbook." St. Louis *Globe-Democrat* 25-26 May 1968.

Wood, Sue Ann. "The Gateway Arch." St. Louis *Globe-Democrat* 17-18 Feb. 1983.

Magazines

Duffy, Robert W. "Joel Meyerowitz—A Photographer Looks at St. Louis." *P-D, The St. Louis Post-Dispatch Sunday Magazine* 15 June 1980: 4-7.

Grey, Jerry. "Expansion into Space." *Environment* Nov. 1983: 40-46.

Hicks, Clifford B. "The Incredible Gateway Arch." *Reader's Digest* March 1964: 169-73.

"Jefferson Memorial Competition Winners." *Architectural Record*, Vol. 103, no. 4 (April 1948).

Louchheim, Aline B. "Now Saarinen the Son." *New York Times Magazine* 26 Apr. 1953: 26, 44-45.

McCall, Louis Marion. "Making St. Louis a Better Place to Live In." *The Chautauquan* Jan. 1903: 405-09.

McGrath, Roger. "Interview: Charles Peterson." *Saint Louis Home* Jan. 1984: 15.

"The Maturing Modern." *Time Magazine* 2 July 1956: 50-57.

"Progress Report: Jefferson National Expansion Memorial Competition Winners Announced." *Progressive Architecture*, Vol. XXIX, no. 3 (March 1948).

Riley, Joseph J. "Arch Rival to the Eiffel." *TWA Ambassador* Sept. 1971: 12-15.

"St. Louis' Gateway Arch." *Steelways* March 1963: 1.

Terry, Dickson. "A Monument to Thirty Years of Patience, Perseverance and Determination." *Missouri Athletic Club Cherry Diamond* Sept. 1964: 25-63.

Vogel-Franzi, Jeanne. "The Fair that Unveiled the Spirit of St. Louis." *Missouri Life* Sept. 1981: 49-52.

Ward, Paul W. "Washington Weekly: $30,000,000 Thomas Jefferson Memorial Project." *The Nation* March 1936: 267-68.

Waterhouse, S. "Missouri—St. Louis, The Commercial Center of North America." *Merchants' Magazine and Commercial Review*. Oct. 1866: 53-61.

Journals

"The City Plan Report of Saint Louis." *Charities and Commons* 19 (Feb. 1908): 1542-45.

Detmers, Bruce; Richard B. Bowser; B.A. Prichard; Fred N. Severud; A.C.Van Tassel, "Jefferson Memorial Arch: A Panel." *Building Research—The Journal of the Building Research Institute* 1.5 (Sept.-Oct. 1964): 58-62.

Jensen, J.E.N. "A Steel Arch...A Symbol of the Spirit of the Pioneers." *Civil Engineering* Oct. 1965.

Jordan, Robert Paul. "St. Louis: New Spirit Soars in Mid-America's proud old city." *National Geographic* 128.5 (Nov. 1965): 605-41.

McQuade, Walter. "Eero Saarinen: A Complete Architect." *Architectural Forum* 115 (Apr. 1962): 103-10.

Saarinen, Aline B. Message read to the convention on the occasion of the awarding of the first Henry Bacon medal for memorial architecture to her late husband for the design of the Gateway Arch. *American Institute of Architects Journal* 46 (Sept. 1966): 68.

"Saarinen feels buildings near St. Louis national arch should not exceed 200 feet—but city rejects idea." *Architectural Forum* 113 (Jul. 1960): 7.

Temko, Allan. "Eero Saarinen:...something between earth and sky..." *Horizon* 2 (Jul. 1960): 77-82, 123-25.

Books

Eero Saarinen on his work. A selection of buildings dating from 1947 to 1964 with statements by the architect, Aline B. Saarinen, ed. New Haven and London: Yale UP, 1962.

Holt, Glen and Troen, Selwyn K., eds. *St. Louis: A Documentary History of American Cities*. New York: Franklin Watts, 1977.

Hosmer, Charles B., Jr. *Preservation Comes of Age, From Williamsburg to the National Trust 1926-1949*. 2 vols. Charlottesville, VA: UP of Virginia, 1981.

Hyde, William and Conrad, Howard L., eds. *Encyclopedia of the History of Saint Louis: A Compendium of History and Biography for Ready Reference*. St. Louis, MO: The Southern History Co., 1899. Vol. 4.

Jefferson, Thomas. "First Inaugural Address." In *An American Primer*. Daniel J. Boorstin, ed. New York: A Mentor Book.

——— "Notes on the State of Virginia." *The American Landscape*. John Conron, ed. New York: Oxford UP, 1973.

McHenry, Estill, ed. *Addresses and Papers of James B. Eads*. St. Louis, MO: Slawson & Co., Printers, 1884.

Meyerowitz, Joel. *St. Louis and the Arch*. Pref. James N. Wood. Boston: New York Graphic Society, 1980.

Saarinen, Eliel. *The city, its growth, its decay, its future*. New York: Reinhold Publishing Corp., 1943.

——— *Search for form: a fundamental approach to art*. New York: Reinhold Publishing Corp., 1948.

Sullivan, Louis H. *The Autobiography of an Idea*. Foreward by Claude Bragdon with a new intro. by Ralph Marlow Line. New York: Dover Publications, 1956.

Whitman, Walt. *Complete Poetry and Collected Prose*. New York: The Library of America, 1982.

Woodward, C.M. *A History of the St. Louis Bridge*. St. Louis: G.I. Jones and Co., 1881.

Secondary Sources

Journals

Bogdanovic, Bogdan. "Symbols in the City and the city as symbol." *Ekistics* 39.232 (Mar. 1975): 140-46.

Brown, Sharon. "Jefferson National Expansion Memorial: The 1947-48 Competition." *Gateway Heritage* 1.3 (Winter 1980): 40-48.

deGraeve, Frank P. "Myth, Literary." *New Catholic Encyclopedia* 10. Prepared by an editorial staff at the Catholic University of America, Washington, D.C. New York: McGraw-Hill (1967): 182-85.

Dos Passos, John. "Builders for a Golden Age." *American Heritage* 10.5 (Aug. 1959): 65-77.

Eisenstadt, Stuart N. "Studies of Modernization and Sociological Theory." *History and Theory* 13.3 (1974): 225-52.

Everhart, William C. "So Long, St. Louis, We're Heading West." *National Geographic* 128.5 (Nov. 1965): 643-69.

Fitch, James Marston. "The Lawn: America's Greatest Architectural Achievement." *American Heritage* 35.4 (June/Jul. 1984): 49-64.

Gies, Joseph. "Mr. Eads Spans the Mississippi." *American Heritage* 20.5 (Aug. 1969): 16-21.

Glassie, Henry. "Meaningful Things and Appropriate Myths: The Artifact's Place in American Studies." *Prospects* 3 (1977): 10-19.

Goering, Karen McCoskey. "Pageantry in St. Louis: The History of the Veiled Prophet Organization." *Gateway Heritage* 4.4 (Spring 1984): 2-16.

Isaac, Erich. "Religion, Landscape, and Space." *Landscape* 9.2 (Winter 1959-60): 14-18.

Jehlen, Myra. "The American Landscape as Totem." *Prospects* 6 (1981) 17-36.

Kouwenhoven, John A. "Eads Bridge: The Celebration." *The Bulletin of the Missouri Historical Society* 30.3 (Apr. 1974): 159-80.

Lombard, John. "Gateway Arch: Catalyst to Downtown Revival." *Saint Louis Business Journal* 20-26 June 1983.

——"Jerry Schober Tells Tales About Monuments." *Saint Louis Business Journal* 20-26 June 1983.

McCue, George. "The Arch: An Appreciation." *Journal of the American Institute of Architects* 67 (1978): 57-63.

Miller, Zane, ed. "City and Suburb." *American Quarterly* 37.3 (1985).

Pressman, Norman E.P. "A planning approach to the study of past urban settlements." *Ekistics* 39.232 (Mar. 1975): 169-71.

Pursell, Carroll W., Jr. "The History of Technology and the Study of Material Culture." *American Quarterly* 35.3 (1983) 304-15.

Rapoport, Amos. "Images, symbols, and popular design." *Ekistics* 39.232 (Mar. 1975) 165-68.

Smith, Peter F. "Symbolic Meaning in Contemporary Cities." *Ekistics* 39.232 (Mar. 1975): 159-64.

Towey, Martin. "Hooverville: St. Louis had the Largest." *Gateway Heritage* 1.2 (Fall 1980): 4-11.

Ward, John Williams. "The Meaning of Lindbergh's Flight." *American Quarterly* 10 (Spring 1958) 3-16.

Wheatley, Paul. "The ancient Chinese city as a cosmological symbol." *Ekistics* 39.232 (Mar. 1975) 147-58.

Wise, Gene. "Paradigm Dramas in American Studies." *American Quarterly* 31 (1979): 293-337.

—— "Some Elementary Axioms for an American Culture Studies." *Prospects* 5 (1979): 517-47.

Woodward, C.M. "The World's First Alloy Steel Bridge." *The Vancoram Review* 14:1 (1958): 8.

Books

Abbey, Edward. *Desert Solitaire: A Season in the Wilderness*. New York: Ballantine Books, 1979.

Agnew, John A., John Mercer and David Sopher. *The City in Cultural Context*. Boston: Allen & Unwin, 1984.

Albanese, Catherine. *Sons of the Fathers*. Philadelphia: Temple UP, 1976.

Ayensu, Edwards S., Vernon H. Heywood, Grenville L. Lucas and Robert A. DeFillipps. *Our Green and Living World: The Wisdom to Save It*. Washington, D.C.: Smithsonian Institution P, 1984.

Bacon, Edmund. *The Design of Cities*. New York: Viking, 1967.

Barthes, Roland. *The Eiffel Tower and Other Mythologies*. Trans. Richard Howard. New York: Hill and Wang, 1979.

Bateson, Gregory. *Steps to an Ecology of Mind.* New York: Ballantine, 1972.

Bellah, Robert, et. al. *Habits of the Heart.* Berkeley, CA: U of California P, 1985.

Berger, Peter and Thomas Luckmanm. *The Social Construction of Reality: A Treatise in the Sociology of Knowledge.* New York: Anchor Books, 1966.

Berry, Wendell. *The Unsettling of America: Culture and Agriculture.* New York: Avon, 1977.

Boorstin, Daniel. *The Americans: The Democratic Experience.* New York: Vintage, 1974.

_____ *The Image: or, What Happened to the American Dream.* New York: Atheneum, 1962.

_____ *The Lost World of Thomas Jefferson.* Boston: Beacon, 1948.

Boulding, Kenneth. "The Economics of the Coming Spaceship Earth." *The Environmental Handbook.* Garrett deBell, ed. New York: Ballantine, 1970.

Boyd, Julian, ed. *The Papers of Thomas Jefferson,* Vol. I. Princeton, NJ: Princeton UP, 1950.

Cassirer, Ernst. *The Logic of the Humanities.* Trans. Clarence Smith Howe. New Haven: Yale UP, 1961.

_____ *The Philosophy of Symbolic Forms.* New Haven: Yale UP, 1957.

Castells, Manuel. *High Technology, Space, and Society.* Urban Affairs Annual Reviews. Beverly Hills, Ca.: Sage Publications, 1983.

Cherry, Conrad, ed. *God's New Israel: Religious Interpretations of American Destiny.* Englewood Cliffs, NJ: Prentice-Hall, 1971.

Chittenden, Hiram H. *The American Fur Trade of the Far West,* Vol. 1. New York: Barnes & Noble, Inc., 1935.

Chudacoff, Howard. *The Evolution of American Urban Society.* New York: Prentice-Hall, 1981.

Clay, Grady. *Close-Up: How to Read the American City.* Chicago: U of Chicago P, 1973.

Deloria, Vine, Jr. *The Metaphysics of Modern Existence.* San Francisco: Harper & Row, 1979.

DeToqueville, Alexis. *Democracy in America.* Philips Bradley, ed. New York: Alfred A. Knopf, 1945. Vol. 1.

Dosch, Donald F. *The Old Courthouse: Americans Build a Forum on the Frontier.* St. Louis: Jefferson National Expansion Memorial Association, 1979.

Eliade, Mircea. *The Sacred and the Profane.* Trans. Willard R. Trask. New York: Harcourt, Brace & World, 1959.

Ellul, Jacques. *The Technological Society.* Trans. John Wilkinson. New York: Vintage, 1964.

Emerson, Ralph Waldo. "The American Scholar." *An American Primer.* Daniel Boorstin, ed. New York: The New American Library, 1968.

Erikson, Erik. *Dimensions of a New Identity.* New York: Norton, 1974.

Fitzgerald, F. Scott. *The Great Gatsby.* New York: Charles Scribner's Sons, 1925.

Gans, Herbert. *The urban villagers.* New York: Free Press of Glencoe, 1962.

Geist, Christopher D. "Historic Sites and Monuments as Icons." *Icons of America*. Ray Browne and Marshall Fishwick, eds. Bowling Green, OH: Popular Press, 1978.

Giedion, Siegfried. *Mechanization Takes Command*. New York: Oxford UP, 1970.

_____ "Symbolic Expression in Prehistory and in the First High Civilizations." *Sign, Image, Symbol*. Gyorgy Kepes, ed. New York: George Braziller, 1966.

Grund, Francis. *The Americans*. Boston, 1837.

Guidoni, Enrico. *Primitive Architecture*. Trans. Robert Erich Wolf. New York: Harry N. Abrams, 1978.

Hofstadter, Richard. *The American Political Tradition and the Men Who Made It*. New York: Vintage, 1948.

Jackson, J.B. "Jefferson, Thoreau and After." *Landscapes*. Ervin H. Zube, ed. Cambridge, MA: U of Massachusetts P, 1970.

_____ "The Order of a Landscape." *The Interpretation of Ordinary Landscapes*. D.W. Meinig, ed. New York: Oxford UP, 1979.

Jacobs, Jane. *The Death and Life of Great American Cities*. New York: Vintage, 1961.

Jencks, Charles. *The Language of Post-Modern Architecture*. New York: Rizzoli International, 1984.

Jung, Carl. *Man and His Symbols*. Garden City, NY: Doubleday, 1964.

Kammen, Michael. *People of paradox: an inquiry into the origins of American civilization*. New York: Oxford UP, 1980.

Kirk, Geoffrey Stephen. *Myth: Its Meaning and Function in Ancient and Other Cultures*. London: Syndics of the Cambridge UP, 1970.

Kouwenhoven, John A. "American Studies: Words or Things?" *Material Culture Studies in America*. Thomas J. Schlereth, ed. Nashville, TN: The American Association for State and Local History, 1982.

Kyvig, David E. and Myron A. Marty. *Nearby History: Exploring the Past Around You*. Nashville, TN: The American Association for State and Local History, 1982.

Levi-Strauss, Claude. *The Savage Mind*. Chicago: U of Chicago P, 1967.

Lowenthal, David. "Age and Artifact: Dilemmas of Appreciation." *The Interpretation of Ordinary Landscapes*. D.W. Meinig, ed. New York: Oxford UP, 1979.

Lowic, Lawrence. *The Architectural Heritage of St. Louis 1803-1891*. St. Louis: Washington University Gallery of Art, 1982.

Marx, Leo. *The Machine in the Garden*. New York: Oxford UP, 1964.

Mead, Sidney. *The nation with the soul of a church*. New York: Harper & Row, 1975.

Mechling, Jay. "Toward an American Ethnophysics." *The Study of American Culture/Contemporary Conflicts*. Luther S. Luedtke. Deland, FL: Everett Edwards, 1977.

Miller, Perry. *American Transcendentalists: Their Prose and Poetry*. Garden City, NY: Doubleday, 1957.

_____ *Nature's Nation*. Cambridge, MA: The Belknap Press of Harvard UP, 1967.

Miller, Zane. *The Urbanization of Modern America: A Brief History*. New York: Harcourt, Brace, Jovanich, 1973.

Morison, Samuel Eliot and Henry Steele Commager. *The Growth of the American Republic.* 2nd vol. New York: Oxford UP, 1962.

Mumford, Lewis. *The city in history: its origins, its transformations, and its prospects.* New York: Harcourt, Brace & World, 1961.

Nash, Roderick. *Wilderness and the American Mind.* New Haven: Yale UP, 1982.

Norberg-Schulz, Christian. *Genius Loci: Towards a Phenomenology of Architecture.* New York: Rizzoli International Publications, 1980.

_____ *Meaning in Western Architecture.* New York: Praeger, 1974

Novak, Barbara. *Nature and Culture: American Landscape and Painting.* New York: Oxford UP, 1980.

Oxford Book of Prayers. George Appleton, ed. New York: Oxford UP, 1985.

Parkes, Henry Bamford. *The American Experience: An Interpretation of the History and Civilization of the American People.* New York: Vintage, 1959.

Peterson, Merrill. *The Jefferson Image in the American Mind.* New York: Oxford UP, 1960.

Potter, David. *People of plenty: economic abundance and the American character.* Chicago: U of Chicago P, 1954.

Primm, James Neal. *Lion of the Valley: St. Louis, Missouri.* Boulder, CO: Pruett, 1981.

Pynchon, Thomas. *Gravity's Rainbow.* New York: Viking, 1973.

Relph, Edward. *Place and Placelessness.* London: Pion Limited, 1976.

Reps, John. *The Making of Urban America: A History of City Planning in the United States.* Princeton, NJ: Princeton UP, 1965.

Robertson, James Oliver. *American Myth, American Reality.* New York: Hill & Wang, 1980.

Schmitt, Peter J. *Back to Nature: The Arcadian Myth In Urban America.* New York: Oxford UP, 1969.

Schorske, Carl. *Fin-de-Siecle Vienna: Politics and Culture.* New York: Alfred A. Knopf, 1980.

Scott, Quinta and Howard S. Miller. *The Eads Bridge.* Columbia, MO: U of Missouri P, 1979.

Scully, Vincent. *American Architecture and Urbanism.* New York: Frederick A. Praeger, 1969.

Smith, E. Baldwin. *Architectural Symbolism of Imperial Rome and the Middle Ages.* Princeton, NJ: Princeton UP, 1956.

Smith, Henry Nash. *Virgin Land: The American West as Symbol and Myth.* Cambridge, MA: Harvard UP, 1970.

Smith, Michael Peter. *The City and Social Theory.* Oxford: Basil Blackwell, 1980.

Sopher, David. "The Landscape of Home." *The Interpretation of Ordinary Landscapes.* D.W. Meinig, ed. New York: Oxford UP, 1979.

Soucie, Gary. "Poisoning the Earth." *The American Land.* Smithsonian Exposition Books. Distributed to the trade by W.W. Norton & Co., New York, 1979.

Spade, Rupert. *Eero Saarinen.* New York: Simon & Schuster, 1971.

Summerson, Sir John. *Heavenly Mansions.* New York: Norton Library, 1963.

_____ "Urban Forms." *The Historian and the City.* Oscar Handlin and John Burchard, eds. Cambridge, MA: The M.I.T. P and Harvard UP, 1963.

Susman, Warren I. *Culture as History: The Transformation of American Society in the Twentieth Century*. New York: Pantheon, 1984.

Tate, Cecil. *The Search for Method in American Studies*. Minneapolis: U of Minnesota P, 1973.

Taylor, Joshua C. *America as Art*. New York: Harper & Row, 1976.

Temko, Allan. *Eero Saarinen*. New York: George Braziller, 1962.

Thrupp, Sylvia L. "The City as the Idea of Social Order." *The Historian and the City*. Oscar Handlin and John Burchard, eds. Cambridge, MA: The M.I.T. P and Harvard UP, The American Association for State and Local History, 1982.

Tuan, Yi-Fu. *Topophilia: A Study of Environmental Perception, Attitudes and Values*. Englewood Cliffs, NJ: Prentice-Hall, 1974.

Tunnard, Christopher and Henry Hope Reed. *American Skyline: The Growth and Form of Our Cities and Towns*. Boston: Houghton Mifflin, 1955.

Tunnard, Christopher. *The City of Man*. New York: Charles Scribner's Sons, 1953.

Venturi, Robert. *Complexity and Contradiction in Architecture*. New York: Museum of Modern Art, 1977.

Wagner, Roy. *The Invention of Culture*. Chicago: U of Chicago P, 1975.

Warner, Sam Bass, Jr. *The Private City: Philadelphia in Three Periods of Its Growth*. Philadelphia: U of Pennsylvania P, 1968.

_____ *The Urban Wilderness: a history of the American City*. New York: Harper & Row, 1972.

Washburn, Wilcomb E. "Manuscripts and Manufacts." *Material Culture Studies in America*. Thomas Schlereth, ed. Nashville, TN: The American Association for State and Local History, 1982.

White, Morton G. and Lucia White. *The Intellectual versus the City, from Thomas Jefferson to Frank Lloyd Wright*. Cambridge, MA: Harvard UP, 1962.

Whitehead, Alfred North. *Symbolism: Its Meaning and Effect*. New York: Capricorn, 1927.

Wiebe, Robert. *The Search for Order, 1877-1920*. 6 vols. *The Making of America* series. David Donald, ed. New York: Hill & Wang, 1967. Vol. 5.

Wittkower, Rudolf. *Palladio and Palladianism*. New York: George Braziller, 1974.

Zaner, Richard. *The Way of Phenomenology: Criticism as a Philosophical Discipline*. Indianapolis: The Bobbs-Merrill Co., 1970.

Zelinsky, Wilbur. *The Cultural Geography of the United States*. Englewood Cliffs, NJ: Prentice-Hall, 1973.